the green Olive tree

RAMON BENNETT

SHEKINAH

Colorado Springs — Jerusalem

All direct quotations within the text proper are enclosed within quotation marks, quotations set off do not require quotation marks. All direct quotations from the Bible are indicated by italics and are enclosed within quotation marks except for quotations set off. All bold emphasis within Bible quotations is the author's own. Proper names and lesser-known foreign words are italicized.

Unless noted otherwise, Scripture quotations are the author's own, translated from the best original texts.

Copyright © 2021, Ramon Bennett

All Rights Reserved

ISBN 978-1-943423-90-3

Written permission must be secured from the author to use or reproduce, by any means, any part of this book, except for brief quotations in reviews or articles.

First printing October 2021

Published and Distributed in the United States by:
Shekinah Books LLC,
755 Engleby Drive, Colorado Springs, Colorado 80930, U.S.A.
Tel: (719) 645-7722. eMail: usa@shekinahbooks.com.
Website: http://www.ShekinahBooks.com.

Distributed in Israel by: Ramon Bennett,
P.O. Box 37111, Jerusalem 91370.
eMail: armofsalvation@mac.com.

Shekinah Books

The printing division of Arm of Salvation Ministriesπ, Jerusalem, Israel.

http://www.shekinahbooks.com

*The L*ORD *called your name,
Green Olive Tree, Lovely and of Good Fruit*
(Jeremiah 11:16).

Dedication

This book is dedicated to the One true God, the Creator and Eternal King of Israel, who gave His chosen people all that they ever had, but who has received so little in return—so few thanks, so little regard or reverence from those to whom He gave and did so much. May the relatively few years left for this world see a quantum shift in the hearts of all Jews. May they come to love Him in the same way as He loves them.

Table of Content

About this book 9
Israel, God's treasured possession 13
The Creation 15
God's disappointment 23
Uniqueness of Israel 33
Abraham, Isaac; and the everlasting covenant 39
Jacob 51
God's fighter 59
Jacob becomes Israel 69
Joseph 73
Joseph in Egypt 77
Joseph and his brothers 85
Israel (Jacob) goes to Egypt 99
Egyptian genocide 107
Moses: A Man of God 113
Moses and Aaron before Pharaoh 123
Catch us if you can 141
Out of the frying pan, into the fire 147
From slavery to bondage 161
A Tabernacle in the Wilderness 165
Twelve spies 183
Forty-year death march 193
Where have all the flowers gone? 199
Cause and Effect 211
Valley of Tears 223
Home at last 235
One like the Son of Man 249
Who is a Jew? 259
The great and terrible Day of the Lord 267

Other book titles by this author 281

About this book

This is a book about Israel, its past, its present and its future. An amount of text, very necessary for understanding the progrssion this book and how much God Almighty did for the patently unappreciative Israelite people, is also necessary for understanding the formation of the ancient state of Israel, including God's "Ten Words," and the statutes pertaining to that time. The magnificent gold-encrusted tabernacle (tabernacle means "tent", hence the many references to "the tent of meeting") and the impressively beautiful vestments for the High Priest and his sons are included in detail and are certainly worth a closer look by readers.

The text throughout strictly adheres to the Bible narrative and follows the best original texts; serving to introduce the main characters and events that led to Israel's foundation. Bible references are interspersed within the text; these indicate where the events take place in the Bible. Important Scripture passages are italicized and offset within the narrative.

Following the initial actions of the players, which led to the founding of the Israel of antiquity, additional passages, each with its new players, are added as historical and moral references until the demise of ancient Israel and its later resurrection as the modern Jewish state. Vignettes, comments, and explanations pertinent to the narrative have been inserted wherever the writer felt it necessary for the reader to gain a better understanding of what is written; these are also enclosed in parenthesis and further offset within the text.

In time, following Jacob's household retinue of seventy-two persons emigrating to Egypt, there arose a king of Egypt, a Pharaoh who did not know of his peoples' debt to Jacob. From that point onward Egypt oppressed the children of Israel and put them under forced labor with hard taskmasters, and they became slaves to Pharaoh, effectively making them the property of Egypt. However, the number of Israelites grew exponentially and the Egyptians became afraid of them. In an act of desperation Pharaoh turned to genocide in a bid to decrease the number of the children of Israel. Initially, the Hebrew midwives were told to to kill every male child when he was born, and when the midwives fabricated a storyline and told Pharaoh that the Hebrew women gave birth before the midwives got to them, Pharaoh ordered all male Hebrew babies be thrown into the Nile and drowned, sparing only the girl babies.

God Almighty used His unparalleled power to crush Egypt with sequential catastrophes until Pharaoh and his people finally exhorted almost two million Israelites to leave the land of Egypt. Once free of Egypt, but in a desert wilderness, the nation-state had to stand up and face the world, but things did not go smoothly for the Israelites. However, the troubles they faced were entirely of their own making. Nothing much has changed since then.

The reader may find some concepts in these pages somewhat unusual for a book about Israel; this is only because God Almighty has long kept some aspects of His salvation hidden in plain sight, awaiting the time and place to reveal them to His children. This book is apparently the time and place for Him to remove some veils from His children's eyes.

This book follows the intense opposition to the reemergence of Israel in the Middle-East and the devastating wars that have been waged against the modern nation. Antisemitism, Jew hatred and anti-Israel mindsets of past and present millennia are, unfortunately, all part of Israel's long and painful history. The book's narrative culminates with the great and terrible *"Day of the LORD"* and the second coming of Yeshua (Jesus), at which point the history of Israel from A to Z ends, along with the end of time as we know it. Now read on.

12

Israel, God's treasured possession

This book, as said earlier, is about Israel, but it is totally unlike any other book about Israel penned by this writer, and perhaps ever penned by any writer. This book is a record of the paradox of Israel from A to Z; it includes all the good, the bad, and the ugly; from before time began until the end of the age and the great and terrible day of the LORD.

It is a well-known fact that Israel and her people are special to God Almighty (אל שדי —please note that Hebrew is read from right to left) and scores of times in the Bible God Almighty portrays Himself as *the Holy One of Israel* and to Israel He says: —

> *The LORD's portion is His people, in Jacob is His inheritance* (Deuteronomy 32:9).
>
> *For you are a people holy to the LORD your God; the LORD your God has chosen you out of all the peoples on earth to be His people, His treasured possession* (Deuteronomy 7:6).

Most of us have at least one treasured possession which we would not part with under any circumstances. Israel is the treasured possession of the Most High God; He said to them: —

> *"You will be a special treasure to me above all peoples on the earth"* (Exodus 19:5).

And:

> *"separate from all the people on the face of the earth"* (Exodus 33:16).
>
> *When the Most High gave the nations their inheritance, When He separated the sons of Adam, He set the boundaries of the peoples according to the*

number of the sons of Israel. For the LORD's *portion is His people; Jacob is the allotment of His inheritance* (Deuteronomy 32:9-10).

In this book the writer has endeavored to peek into the mind of the LORD God— *"the Holy One of Israel"* —in order to get some understanding of why and how far back in time Israel was precious in the heart of God Almighty, and why He warns the world when He says of Israel: *"whoever touches you touches the pupil of My eye"* (Zechariah 2:8).

> (All popular English translations apart from NET render the Hebrew here—בבבת עינו—as *"touches the apple of His eye,"* but it literally means *"pokes a finger in the pupil of His eye,"* which is more than touching God Almighty's favorite; it is harming God's most delicate, sensitive organ, that when seen up really close mirrors the images before it and must be meticulously guarded at all times. And so throughout this book.)

Israel is also a blessed nation:—

Blessed is the nation whose God is the LORD, *the people He has chosen as His own inheritance* (Psalms 33:12).

When other nations have crumbled into dust Israel has been, and will be in the future, left standing, because the Israelis are the *"people of the* LORD*"* and is the LORD God's own inheritance among the peoples of this planet:—

Not like these is the LORD, *the portion of Jacob, for He is the one who formed all things, and Israel is the tribe of His inheritance; the* LORD *of armies is His name* (Jeremiah 10:16).

The Creation

The Bible informs us that, *"In the beginning God created...."* (Genesis 1:1). God Almighty is the Great Creator; He *created the heavens and the earth and the seas and everything in them.* Then *God commanded light to shine out of darkness* and said: —

Let there be light"; and there was light (Genesis 1:3). And *God separated the light from the darkness, the light He called Day, and the darkness He called Night* (Genesis 1:5).

From that we begin to see and understand the super-miraculous power of God Almighty. The best humans can do is to shine light ***into*** darkness, but God Almighty commanded light to shine ***out*** of darkness. Humans have never duplicated that feat. And we see that God Almighty's Word is individually creative; and the Apostle John elucidates: —

In the beginning was the Word, and the Word was with God, and the Word was God. He was in the beginning with God. All things were made through him, and without him was not any thing made that was made (John 1:1–3).

And now we see more of the miraculous; the sterile environment that defined our planet was empowered to bring forth life via seed-yielding vegetation and fruit-bearing trees: —

*God said, "**Let the earth sprout** vegetation, plants yielding seed, and fruit trees bearing fruit in which is their seed, each according to its kind, on the earth." And it was so. The earth brought forth vegetation, plants yielding seed according to their own kinds,* *and trees bearing fruit in which is their seed, each according to its kind* (Genesis 1:11–12).

Out of the ground the L*ORD* *God made every tree grow that is pleasant to the sight and good for food. The tree of life was also in the middle of the garden, and* **the tree of the knowledge of good and evil**

(Genesis 2:9).

Then God Almighty went ahead and filled the heavens and the seas with living creatures; and these are truly *creatures* because they were *created*:—

*God said, "**Let the waters bring forth** swarms of living creatures, and let birds fly above the earth across the dome of the sky." So **God created** the great sea monsters and every living creature that moves, of every kind, with which the waters swarm, and every winged bird of every kind* (Genesis 1:20–21).

And the earth was empowered to bring forth living creatures, animals of every kind:—

*God said, "**Let the earth bring forth** living creatures of every kind: cattle and creeping things and wild animals of the earth of every kind." And it was so*

(Genesis 1:24).

Then God Almighty made a quantum leap and made Man (humans), not after its own kind, but in the image and likeness of Himself:—

*God said, "**Let us** (God Almighty and the Word) **make** Man in our image, after our likeness. And let them have dominion over the fish of the sea and over the birds of the heavens and over the livestock and over all the earth and over every creeping thing that creeps on the earth."*

The Creation

So God created Man in his own image, in the image of God he created him; male and female he created them.

And God blessed them. And God said to them, "Be fruitful and multiply and fill the earth and subdue it, and have dominion over the fish of the sea and over the birds of the heavens and over every living thing that moves on the earth" (Genesis 1:26–28).

The earth could have brought forth humans, had it been so instructed, just like it had brought forth the animals and cattle, and the birds that filled the heavens, like the seas had brought forth fish and great sea monsters, but Man was formed from the ground by the fingers of God Almighty, in His own image, after His own likeness. Humans, therefore, have the ability to create and to reason; which are but two of the many differences between humans and other created flesh:—

The LORD God formed Man from the dust of the ground, and breathed into his nostrils the breath of life; and the Man became a living being

(Genesis 2:7).

God Almighty made Man in His own image and likeness, and He made him male and female, making no provision for any LGBTQ+ nonsense, which appears to be the mode in this present godless age for *"God is not the author of confusion"* (1Corinthians 14:33), His creation was perfect. The Bible has much to say against homosexuality and sodomy; "trans" folk are also anathema to God Almighty:—

A woman shall not wear a man's apparel, nor shall a man put on a woman's garment; for whoever does such things is abhorrent to the LORD your God

(Deuteronomy 22:5).

After He had made Man from the dust of the ground God Almighty breathed into Man's nostrils the breath of life:—

God is Spirit, and those who worship Him must worship in spirit and truth (John 4:24)

Therefore, with God Almighty being Spirit, the *breath of life* that He breathed into Man was nothing less than the Holy Spirit—like when the resurrected Yeshua (Jesus) breathed on his disciples and said, *"Receive the Holy Spirit"* (John 20:22)—which places humans far above all else that had been created.

The Man gave names to all cattle, and to the birds of the air, and to every animal of the field; but for the Man there was not found a helper as his partner. So the LORD God caused a deep sleep to fall upon the Man, and while he slept took one of his ribs and closed up its place with flesh. And the rib that the LORD God had taken from the Man he made into a woman and brought her to the Man. Then the Man said, "This at last is bone of my bones and flesh of my flesh; she will be called Woman, because she was taken out of Man" (Genesis 2:20–23).

> (The LORD God did not permanently remove the male's rib, He just used the bone to fashion the female of the species. Both sexes have the same number of ribs.)

A Woman is a female Man, she is not a different species, therefore the term "chairman" applies to both male and female. A female Man is in no wise inferior to a male Man, albeit generally she has a smaller skeleton, shorter limbs, and thinner and weaker bones than the male, which makes it extremely unfair for a biological male to compete against biological females in athletic sports events.

The Creation

A female Man has a God-given function; she was specifically made as a *"helper,"* a *"partner"* for the male (Genesis 2:18), but she is not inferior to the male of the species, she is merely weaker in bone and muscle strength. Man and his Woman were given equal opportunity in the job of tending the garden of Eden and there was only one rule: they must not eat of the fruit of the tree of the knowledge of good and evil or they will die:—

> *The LORD God took Man and put them in the garden of Eden to till it and keep it. And the LORD God commanded Man, "You may freely eat of every tree of the garden; but of the tree of the knowledge of good and evil you will not eat, for in the day that you eat of it you will surely die"* (Genesis 2:9).

However, humans are *"born to trouble just as sparks fly upward"* (Job 5:7). Taking a stroll around the garden the couple encountered a serpent, a snake, who was the most crafty of all the animals of the creation:—

> *The Woman told the serpent, "We may eat of the fruit of the trees in the garden; but God Almighty said, 'You will not eat of the fruit of the tree that is in the middle of the garden, nor will you touch it, or you will die'"* (Genesis 3:4b–5).

> *But the serpent said to the Woman, "You will not die; for God knows that when you eat of it your eyes will be opened, and you will be like God, knowing good and evil"* Genesis 3:4).

> *And when the woman saw that the tree was good for food, and that it was a delight to the eyes, and that the tree was to be desired to make one wise, she took of its fruit and ate; and she also gave some to her husband, who was with her, and he ate* (Genesis 3:8).

And so we have the first example of *"the lust of the flesh, the lust of the eyes, the pride of life"* (1John 2:16) and it caused the fall of Man. The crafty serpent knew that Man and his Woman would not physically die by disobeying God Almighty's command not to eat of the fruit of *the tree of the knowledge of good and evil,* but the moment they bit into the fruit of that tree they died spiritually. And since that day every descendant of that first couple have been born *"dead in trespasses and sins"* (Ephesians 2:1).

It was not long before God Almighty moved to address Mans' disobedience and, as soon as Man heard God's footsteps, they hid themselves among the trees in the garden. Then the LORD God called to the Man, *"Where are you?"*

> (Here the LORD God was asking a rhetorical question. God Almighty's attributes include being omnipresent, omnipotent, and omniscient, which means He well knew where Man and his Woman were. God was simply opening up a dialogue with His Man creation who was hiding from Him.)

And the Man said, *"I heard the sound of you in the garden and was afraid because I was naked."* And the LORD God said *"Who told you that you were naked? Have you eaten from the tree which I commanded you not to eat?"* And then the blame games began.

The Man said: —

> **The Woman** *whom you gave to be with me, she gave me fruit from the tree, and I ate* (Genesis 3:12).

Then the LORD God said to the Woman, *"What is this you have done?"* And the Woman said, *"**The serpent** tricked me, and I ate."* (Genesis 3:13).

And the Lord God said to the serpent:—
Because you deceived Man and have done great harm:—

> *cursed are you among all animals and among all wild creatures; upon your belly you will go, and dust you will eat all the days of your life"*
> (Genesis 3:14).

(Only a few people seem to be aware that inside every serpent (snake) are four atrophied legs. Serpents originally walked like animals and ate grass and similar types of food. When God Almighty curses something or someone there are dire consequences:—

> *Woe to the world because of the things that cause people to stumble! Such things must come, but woe to the person through whom they come!"*
> (Matthew 18:7.)

To the Woman the Lord God said:—

> *I will greatly increase your pains in childbearing; in pain you will bring forth children, yet your desire will be for your husband, and he will rule over you* (Genesis 3:16).

(The intense pain of childbirth for a woman is the consequence of the first Woman's disobedience.)

Then to the Man the Lord God said:—
> *Because you have listened to the voice of your wife, and have eaten of the tree about which I ommanded you, 'You shall not eat of it', cursed*

> *is the ground because of you; in toil you will eat of it all the days of your life; thorns and thistles it will bring forth for you; and you will eat the plants of the field. By the sweat of your brow you will eat bread until you return to the ground, for out of it you were taken; you are dust, and to dust you will return*
> (Genesis 3:17–19).

> (The thorns and thistles that plague all our lands and tear our flesh is a consequence of the first Man's disobedience.)

God Almighty was not fazed by Mans' disobedience in the garden. We read in Genesis 3:21 that God Almighty *"made garments from skin for Adam and his wife, and clothed them."* This is the first intimation that sacrifice was necessary to atone for Mans' sin. The LORD God had long before foreseen the sinfulness of Man and had personally planned for Man's ultimate redemption. Everything has taken time, and will continue to take time throughout the millennia-long human history before it becomes actual, but God Almighty's plans for Man transcends all time:—

> *In this is love, not that we loved God but that he loved us and sent His Son to be the atoning sacrifice for our sins* (1John 4:10).

God's disappointment

Obviously, God Almighty had given things an amount of thought before making the Earth, the heavens, the seas, and Man. He had a plan in place before He even began generating His creation. God Almighty knew from the beginning that humans would disappoint (placing *"the tree of the knowledge of good and evil in the middle of the garden"* (Genesis 2:9) where Man could not miss it would have been by God's choice, not by chance) and the LORD God would not have been taken by surprise that within ten generations it is chronicled:—

> *God Almighty saw that the wickedness of man was great in the earth, and that every intention of the thoughts of his heart was only evil continually. And the LORD regretted that He had made Man on the earth, and it grieved him to His heart* (Genesis 6:5–6).

Decent, moral, God-fearing men and women were no less at a premium in the days of yore than they are today. We read of Enoch, the sixth from Adam (the first Man), who walked with God. Enoch was so pleasing to God that he never died, God translated him, took him straight home to heaven while he was yet living (Genesis 5:24).

Noah was the tenth generation from Adam, and it is recorded that Noah *"found favor in the eyes of God"* (Genesis 6:8) and God Almighty said to Noah: *"I have seen that **you alone are righteous** before me in this generation"* (Genesis 7:1) and He decided to use Noah in His purposes, which was to wipe the slate clean and start over with humans and all living, breathing reptiles, animals and birds, whose habitat was the land, the forests and the air:—

Now the earth was corrupt in God's sight, and the earth was filled with violence (Genesis 6:11).

And God said to Noah, "I have determined to make an end of all flesh, for the earth is filled with violence because of them; now I am going to destroy them along with the earth" (Genesis 6:13).

God Almighty had Noah build a huge Ark, a sanctuary ship of cypress wood with three floors and rooms large enough to hold seven pairs of male and female of every living, breathing clean creation, and of the unclean two males and their females, together with sufficient food to sustain everything and everyone in Noah's family of eight persons for an undetermined length of time.

Without help, other than from his family, and no doubt amid a lot of jeering, sneering and mocking from his neighbors, Noah completed the Ark and its provisioning; and God Almighty said:—

After seven more days I will cause it to rain on the earth for forty days and forty nights, and I will wipe from the face of the ground every living thing that I have made (Genesis 7:4).

Noah, his wife and their sons—Shem, Ham, and Japheth—along with their wives, entered the sanctuary Ark and Noah had all the animals come two by two into the ark as God Almighty had commanded, and then God Almighty "closed them in" (Genesis 7:16).

(It is interesting to note that many English translations of the Bible have God Almighty telling Noah and his family to "*go into the Ark*," whereas the Hebrew text definitely says "*come into the Ark*." This would suggest that there was a good deal of interaction between Noah and the LORD and that the LORD was actually in the Ark telling Noah to "come into the Ark." The NKJV and NET Bible have translated it correctly, exactly as it is in the Hebrew text.)

After rain began it fell for forty days and nights and flooding prevailed. It lifted the Ark up until it floated on the surface of the flood. The waters greatly prevailed and kept increasing until all the mountains were submerged and every living, breathing thing that moved upon the earth died, everything that breathed the spirit of life through its nostrils. The waters prevailed over all things for one hundred and fifty days, only Noah and those with him in the Ark survived.

After one hundred and fifty days God Almighty caused a wind to blow over the waters, and they slowly subsided. On the seventeenth day of the seventh month the Ark came to rest on the mountains of Ararat and some weeks later—on the first day of the tenth month—the tops of the mountains were visible. About five weeks later Noah opened the window and let out a raven, but it found no place to rest and just flew up and down. Another week passed and Noah sent out a dove but it returned, finding no place to rest. A further seven days passed and Noah sent the dove out again and this time it came back with an olive leaf in its beak, Noah then knew the water had subsided. Seven months after the Ark had rested on the mountains of Arafat, the earth's surface was finally dry.

(We should here take note of the day and the month on which the Ark rested on the mountains of Ararat, because it is a recurring date that ushered in both salvation for all mankind and fresh returns to godliness for the people of Israel. Yeshua (Jesus) was crucified on the fourteenth day of the first month of the Hebrew year, which was *Aviv*—now called *Nisan* and rose from the dead on the seventeenth day of that first month; however, before God Almighty made the calendar change the first month of the Hebrew year was *Tishrei*, which was the seventh month. So, when the Ark came to rest of the mountains of Ararat on the seventeenth day of the seventh month, it actually came to rest on the same day that Yeshua (Jesus) was resurrected. Thus for Noah and his family, that date brought salvation and Scripture bears witness to it: *"God waited patiently in the days of Noah, during the building of the Ark, in which a few, that is, eight persons, were saved through water and this water symbolizes baptism that now saves you"* (1Peter 3:20–21). We will keep abreast of such dates as this book progresses.)

God Almighty spoke to Noah and told him to take his family and every living thing with him out of the Ark so that all could breed abundantly, filling and replenishing the earth. So Noah left the sanctuary ship with his wife and his sons and their wives and every thing went out by their families and God Almighty said to them: *"Be fruitful and multiply on the earth."*

The LORD said in his heart, "I will never again curse the ground because of Man, for the intention of Man's heart is evil from his youth. Neither will I ever again strike down every living creature as I have done" (Genesis 8:21).

Despite God Almighty's personal disappointment in Man and Mans' almost complete exit from the world scene, God had made provision for Man's fall even before creating him; the LORD had clear plans for spreading righteousness across the face of the earth.

We need to understand that Yeshua (Jesus), the Messiah (Christ), the Anointed One, was preordained by God Almighty to suffer death for Mans' sins even before the creation of the world (1Peter 1:20), and those whom God Almighty chose to receive forgiveness of sins and inherit eternal life are called *"the elect"* and were also preordained before the creation of the world; they were chosen:—

in Messiah (Christ) before the foundation of the world to be holy and blameless before him in love (Ephesians 1:4), *in whom we have redemption, the forgiveness of sins* (Colossians 1:14).

Which is a sea change from the heart of Man that brought about the flood and caused the death of all living things. But, as said earlier, everything in Mans' world takes time before it becomes actual.

It took ten generations of Man to produce righteous Noah, and it took another ten generations to produce righteous Abram, later named Abraham, whom God Almighty called *"My friend"* (Isaiah 41:8). Abram walked with God (Genesis 48:15), but he was childless because his wife Sarai was barren. However, God Almighty came to Abram in a vision and brought him outside and said:—

Look toward heaven, and number the stars, if you are able to number them. Then He said to him, "So will your offspring be." Abram believed the LORD, and He credited it to him as righteousness (Genesis 15:5–6).

And then the LORD God said to Abram:—

No longer will your name be called Abram, but your name will be Abraham, for I have made you the father of many nations (Genesis 17:5).

Then the LORD God said to Abraham:

As for Sarai your wife, you will not call her Sarai, but Sarah (Princess) will be her name. I will bless her, and moreover I will give you a son by her. I will bless her, and she will give rise to nations; kings of peoples will come from her (Genesis 17:15–16).

The righteousness that God Almighty was looking for in Man came through Abraham; and all of Mankind who had faith like that of Abraham would be deemed righteous by God. It was not that Abraham *believed in* God, but that he actually *believed God*, and there is a big difference between believing *in* and actually believing God. Abraham is the father of faith and it is through the descendants of his son Isaac—the son of promise—that the true *"Israel of God"* would begin to emerge.

Some may opine that it is unreasonable to expect humans to believe in a Creator God who is not normally seen. However, Noah deeply believed, built an Ark, saved his family and all living creatures. Abram, too, deeply believed and was given all the land of Canaan, which his descendants inherited; other righteous persons also believed. Why was that? They saw the obvious, understood and believed: —

> *Ever since the creation of the world God Almighty's eternal power and divine nature, invisible though they are, have been understood and seen through the things He has made. So they are without excuse*
> (Romans 1:20).

It is a question of faith. God Almighty has always been. He has no beginning and He has no end; but the incredible works of His creation are all around us. They are there for us to see and enjoy and when we really 'see' then we will also believe. Instead of having faith in an Almighty Creator God, many, as the ancients did, choose to place their life and wellbeing in a material object, even a stone or an idol, none of which can either see or hear nor bring anything into existence.

In the eyes of God Almighty, being righteous means having implicit faith in God Almighty, accompanied by actions that attest to having such faith. Both Noah and Abraham possessed this type of faith and were declared righteous by the LORD because of it. Phinehas, the grandson of Aaron the High Priest, showed, by his actions, that he was zealous for the name of the LORD and was also declared righteous by his God. The actions of Phinehas were recorded for posterity: —

> *While Israel was staying at Shittim, the people began to have sexual relations with the women of Moab. These invited the people to the sacrifices of their gods, and the people ate and bowed down to their gods. Thus Israel yoked itself to the Baal*

of Peor, and the LORD's *anger was kindled against Israel. The* LORD *said to Moses, "Take all the chiefs of the people, and impale them in the sun before the* LORD, *in order that the fierce anger of the* LORD *may turn away from Israel." And Moses said to the judges of Israel, "Each of you will kill any of your people who have yoked themselves to the Baal of Peor".*

Just then one of the Israelites came and brought a Midianite woman into his family, in the sight of Moses and in the sight of the whole congregation of the Israelites, while they were weeping at the entrance of the tent of meeting. When Phinehas son of Eleazar, son of Aaron the priest, saw it, he got up and left the congregation. Taking a spear in his hand, he went after the Israelite man into the tent, and pierced the two of them, the Israelite and the woman, through the belly. So the plague was stopped among the people of Israel. Nevertheless those that died by the plague were twenty-four thousand (Numbers 25:1–9).

Phinehas stood up and intervened, and the plague was stopped. And that was reckoned to him as righteousness from generation to generation forever
(Psalms 106:30-31).

And for his action God Almighty praised Phinehas:—
Phinehas son of Eleazar, son of Aaron the priest, has turned back My wrath from the Israelites by manifesting such zeal among them on My behalf that in My jealousy I did not consume the Israelites
(Numbers 25:11).

God's disappointment   31

However, God Almighty made a promise to the people of Israel through the prophet Isaiah that, in the latter days, *"Your people will all be righteous; ...in its time I will hasten it"* (Isaiah 60:21a, 22b), which is a nod to Romans:—

And so all Israel will be saved; as it is written, "Out of Zion will come the Deliverer; He will remove ungodliness from Jacob" (Romans 11:26),

32

Uniqueness of Israel

The nation of Israel and the people of Israel are unique in many ways. As a nation, Israel was born outside of its land, and its people became slaves—free foreign labor for Egypt and the Egyptians abused and exploited them for decades, perhaps centuries. The Egyptian slavers were initially more numerous than the enslaved children of Israel and the Egyptian masters had both governing and military powers, whereas the enslaved only had each other and the clothes that they wore, but they had God Almighty on their side.

The real beginning of the story of Israel is in upper Mesopotamia, in Ur of the Chaldeans, which today is in southern Iraq. *Ur* is the moon goddess and *Chaldee* (*Khaldi*) means *moon worshiper*.

An Eberite, then named Abram, lived in Ur with his wife, then named Sarai, and his father, Terah. Sarai was barren, she had no child. Abram's brother, Haran, died in Ur and Abram took his orphaned nephew Lot, Haran's son, under his wing. Together they set out to travel to the land of Canaan, but they only journeyed about six hundred miles (nine hundred and sixty-six kilometers) to Haran, which is in present-day Turkey, and they settled there. Abram's father Terah died there.

According to a renowned Midrash (rabbinic interpretation of the biblical text), Abram began his journey from Haran to Canaan by first smashing the idols that his father Terah manufactured in his workshop and then sold. This led Abram—later known as Abraham—to become the first monotheist in the world and we begin to understand why God Almighty chose him as an essential tool in reforming His world.

In Haran God Almighty spoke to Abram / Abraham and told him to leave his family home and his country and travel to another land which the LORD would show him.

God Almighty told Abram / Abraham that He would bless him and make from him a great nation; that Abraham's name would be great and that He would bless all those who blessed Abraham and would curse all those who dishonored Abraham, and that in Abraham all the families of the earth would be blessed (Genesis 12:1–3):—

The promises were made to Abraham and his Seed. Scripture does not say, "And to seeds," as of many, but as of one, "and to your Seed," who is Messiah (Christ) — (Galatians 3:16).

As we saw earlier, God Almighty had a plan for Man that even preceded time itself. Abraham was part of that plan and Abraham's *Seed*, Christ, the Jewish Messiah, the *"Lamb of God,"* who would bring blessing to all the families of the earth, was slain before the creation of the world (Revelation 13:8). And the true descendants of Abraham are those of the seed of Isaac, who was the son of promise:—

For not all Israelites truly belong to Israel, and not all of Abraham's children are his true descendants; but "It is through Isaac that descendants will be named for you." This means that it is not the children of the flesh who are the children of God, but the children of the promise are counted as descendants
(Romans 9:6–8).

Ishmael was a descendant of Abraham as were Ishmael's descendants. However, Ishmael was before Isaac and so he and his descendants are *"children of the flesh,"* not *"children of the promise";* therefore Scripturally they are not *"children of God"* (Romans 9:8).

Abraham was an Eberite, being a descendent of Eber; however, Abraham was six times removed from Eber so he was only a distant relation, but the whole region in Mesopotamia where they had lived was called Eber, and from Eber we get the word "Hebrew," but it is not clear whether Abraham was called a "Hebrew" (Genesis 14:13) because he was an Eberite and a distant relation of Eber, or because he came from the region of Eber.

Abraham journeyed to Canaan with his wife Sarah, his servants, his livestock and his nephew Lot. God Almighty appeared to Abraham while he was still childless and said, *"To your descendants I will give this land"* (Genesis 12:7). And Abraham built an altar there to the LORD God who had appeared to him.

> (Abraham was a true worshiper of God Almighty and six different times—Genesis 12:7, 12:8, 13:18, 22:9, 26:25, 35:7—we read that he *"built an altar to the LORD."* Other prominent men of God also expressed their feelings and dedication to God Almighty by building altars—Noah, Isaac, Jacob (Israel), Moses, Aaron, Joshua, Gideon, Samuel, Saul, David and Elijah.)

Abraham was *"very rich in livestock, in silver and in gold"* (Genesis 13:2) and Lot also had *"flocks and herds and tents"* (Genesis 13:5) and the land could not sustain them together, because their possessions were so great. Of a consequence, friction and disagreement broke out between the herdsmen of Abraham's livestock and the herdsmen of Lot's livestock.

Abraham said to Lot: —

> *Let there not be strive between you and me and between your herdsmen and my herdsmen for we are kindred. Look, is not the whole land before you? Please separate from me. If you go to the left I will go to the right, or if to the right I will go to the left. Lot looked about him, and saw that the plain of the Jordan was well watered everywhere like the garden of the Lord, like the land of Egypt, in the direction of Zoar; this was before the Lord had destroyed Sodom and Gomorrah. So Lot chose for himself all the plain of the Jordan, and Lot journeyed eastward; thus they separated from each other*
>
> (Genesis 13:7–11).

Lot should have been indebted and morally obligated to his uncle Abraham who had been the source of his wealth, but he had no compunction about taking the very best of the land for himself; and here began Lot's downward economic and spiritual spirals. Separated from Abraham, who was under God Almighty's care, Lot was bereft of his uncle's goodness, wisdom and godly guidance and his fortunes rapidly declined. Lot went left toward the Jordan valley, which was like the garden of the Lord, but ended up domiciled in godless Sodom, a city that in due course God Almighty destroyed, along with some other neighboring wicked and profane cities, because of all their evils. God-fearing Abraham went to the right and continued being blessed by the Lord, all of which presents us with an example of liberal left and religious right. The reason Abraham would allow Lot to take the best of the land was because God Almighty had deeded all the land of Canaan to Abraham and his descendants, forever. Lot was not a descendant of Abraham therefore the land would in due time return back to Abraham and his descendants.

There came a war in the region. Nine kings and their armies fought one another—four kings against five, in the Valley of Siddim where there were many tar pits. The kings of Sodom and Gomorrah fled from before their opponents and some of their men fell into the tar pits while the rest fled into the hills for safety. The victorious kings carried off all the goods and provisions of their foe and all that of Sodom and Gomorrah, and went on their way; they also carried off Lot and his possessions since he lived in Sodom (Genesis 14:10–13).

When Abraham heard that his nephew had been taken prisoner he mustered his trained men (318) and, along with some allies, went after the four triumphant kings as far as Dan. Abraham divided his forces against the enemy and routed them, pursuing them as far as Hobah, which is north of Damascus. Abraham recovered all the plundered goods, along with his nephew Lot and his goods, and all the men and women taken captive by the four kings (Genesis 14:14–16).

After Abraham's return from the defeat of the kings, the king of Sodom went out to meet him at the King's Valley, and King Melchizedek of Salem brought out bread and wine; Melchizedek was priest of God Most High. He blessed Abraham and said:—

Blessed be Abraham by God Most High, maker of heaven and earth; and blessed be God Most High, who has delivered your enemies into your hand!
(Genesis 14:19).

Abraham gave Melchizedek, King of Salem, one tenth of all the goods be had recovered. Then the king of Sodom said to Abraham, "Give me the people, but take the goods for yourself." However, Abraham said to the king of Sodom, "I have sworn to the LORD, God Most High, maker of heaven and earth, that I would not take a thread or a sandal-thong or anything that is yours, so that you cannot say, 'I have made Abraham rich.' I will take nothing but what the young men have eaten, and the share of the men who went with me—Aner, Eshcol, and Mamre. Let them take their share" (Genesis 14:17–24).

> (Of this Melchizedek, who has briefly entered upon the stage of our Israel drama, we know very little. He is a mystery of God Almighty. He is an enigma wrapped in a riddle. We know that the name Melchizedek means *"King of Righteousness"* and that his being king of Salem means he is *"King of Peace."* We are informed that:—
>
> > *he is without father or mother or genealogy, having neither beginning of days nor end of life, but resembling the Son of God he continues a priest forever* (Hebrews 7:3).
>
> The only other mention of this divine character is in a Messianic reference in Psalms where God Almighty swears on oath that Yeshua (Jesus) is a priest according to the order of Melchizedek:—
>
> > *The LORD has sworn and will not relent: "You are a priest forever according to the order of Melchizedek"*
> >
> > (Psalms 110:4).

Abraham, Isaac; and the everlasting covenant

Even though Lot had taken the most fertile land in Canaan his wealth and assets had decreased until all that he had left was his home in Sodom, which was a wicked city in God's sight, where many of the people were homosexual and sodomites. Sodom is the home of the word sodomite, a person who sodomizes another:—

Sodom and Gomorrah and the surrounding cities, indulged in sexual immorality and pursued unnatural lust, serve as an example and underwent a punishment of eternal fire (Jude 7).

So evil was the city that God Almighty decided to erase it from the face of the earth. The LORD remembered His friend Abraham and spared Lot and his family when two angels came to destroy Sodom and the surrounding cities. It was necessary for the angels to virtually drag Lot, his wife and his daughters out of Sodom and Lot's wife disobeyed the angels' command of, "Do not look back," but looked back at *"the city burning with fire and brimstone from heaven and she turned into a pillar of salt"* (Genesis 19:24–26).

Lot took shelter in a cave in the mountains and his daughters, fearing they were the only humans left on earth, got him drunk with wine and lay with him incestuously; the eldest daughter on the first night and the younger daughter the following night. Lot was so drunk that he did not know when either of his daughters lay down with him or when they got up, but both girls became pregnant by their father. The eldest daughter gave birth to a son whom she named Moab, and he became the father of the Moabites. The younger daughter also gave birth to a son whom she named Ben-ammi, and he became the father of Ammon (Genesis 19:32–38). These children, born from a drunken, incestuous union, were the fathers of the Moabite and Ammonite tribes; two of the most wicked tribes told in the Bible.

Then God Almighty took note of Abraham's wife Sarah (formerly Sarai), and did for her as He had promised, so Sarah conceived and bore a son to Abraham in his old age. Abraham called his son's name Isaac and circumcised him on the eighth day as God Almighty had commanded him. Abraham was one hundred years old (Genesis 21:5) when Isaac was born to him, and Sarah was ninety years old (Genesis 17:17) when she gave birth.

> (We saw earlier in the piece that God Almighty would *"send His Son to be the atoning sacrifice for our sins* (1John 4:10). The *Son* of course was Yeshua (Jesus) and in Abraham's willingness to offer up his only son Isaac, we see a forerunner of what took place at Calvary aeons later.
>
> When Isaac was in his teen years God Almighty tested Abraham's faith and commitment to Him. He called to him, "Abraham!" And Abraham responded with, "Here I am." And God Almighty said, "Take now your *beloved son*, your *only son* Isaac, and go to the land of Moriah and *offer him* there as a burnt offering on one of the mountains, on *a mountain that I will show you.*" So Abraham rose early in the morning, saddled his donkey,

Abraham, Isaac; and the everlasting covenant

and taking two young men, together with his son Isaac, they split the wood for the burnt offering and set out for a place in the distance that God had shown him. On *the third day* Abraham looked and saw the place far away. Then he said to his young men, "Stay here with the donkey; the lad and I will go over there and *we will worship, then we will come back to you*." Abraham took the wood for the burnt offering and laid it on his son Isaac. Abraham himself carried the fire and the knife. As they both walked on together. Isaac said to his father Abraham, "Father!" And Abraham said, "Here I am, my son." Isaac said, "The fire and the wood are here, but where is the lamb for the burnt offering?" Abraham replied, "*God Almighty sees Himself the lamb* for the burnt offering, my son." And they both walked on together.

When they came to the place that God had shown him, Abraham built an altar and laid the wood in order on it. Abraham then bound his son Isaac, and laid him on the altar, on top of the wood. Abraham then reached out and took the knife to slay his son. However, the Angel of the Lord called to him from heaven, and said, "Abraham, Abraham!" And Abraham said, "Here I am." The Angel said, "Do not lay your hand on the lad or do anything to him; for now I know that you fear Me, since you have not withheld your son, *your only son*, from Me." Abraham looked up and saw a ram, caught in a thicket by its horns. Abraham took the ram and offered it up as a burnt offering instead of his son. So Abraham called that place *"The LORD will see"*; as it is said to this day, *"On the mount of the LORD it will be seen"* (Genesis 22:1–14).

For the three days that they traveled to reach Mount Moriah, Isaac was as good as dead. Abraham considered slaying his only son an act of worship. Abraham believed in a resurrection because he said to his young men, *"we will worship and come back to you."* We see no more of Isaac until he takes his bride (Genesis 24:66), just as we see no more of Yeshua (Jesus) until he comes from heaven to take *the Israel of God* as his bride.

Many English translations in the above passage has it that "the LORD will provide," and that the place was named "In the mount of the LORD it will be provided." This is incorrect; it should be, *"the LORD sees Himself the lamb"* — as Yeshua (Jesus) said, *"I and the Father are one"* (John 10:30), and of course it was at Calvary, which is Mount Moriah, that the crucifixion of God Almighty's only Son was *seen*.)

After Lot had separated from Abraham God Almighty came to Abraham again, and said: —

Abraham, Isaac; and the everlasting covenant

Lift up your eyes and look from the place where you are, northward and southward and eastward and westward, for all the land that you see I will give to you and to your offspring forever. I will make your offspring as the dust of the earth, so that if one can count the dust of the earth, your offspring also can be counted. Arise, walk through the length and the breadth of the land, for I will give it to you
                    (Genesis 13:14–17).

Later, God Almighty appeared to Abraham again, and said to him:—

I am the LORD *who brought you from Ur of the Chaldees, to give you this land to possess. But he said, "O* LORD *God, how am I to know that I will possess it?" He said to him, 'Bring me a heifer three years old, a female goat three years old, a ram three years old, a turtledove, and a young pigeon.' He brought him all these and cut them in two, laying each half over against the other; but he did not cut the birds in two. And when birds of prey came down on the carcasses, Abraham drove them away.*

As the sun was going down, a deep sleep fell upon Abraham, and a deep and terrifying darkness descended upon him. Then the LORD *said to Abraham, "Know this for certain, that your offspring will be aliens in a land that is not theirs, and will be slaves there, and they will be oppressed for four hundred years; but I will bring judgment on the nation that they serve, and afterward they will come out with great possessions. As for yourself, you will go to your ancestors in peace; you will be buried at a good old age. And they will come back here in the fourth generation; for the iniquity of the Amorites is not yet complete"* (Genesis 15:7–16).

(We should here note a few things: The first is that it is wrongly believed by millions of Christians and erroneously taught from pulpits everywhere that a biblical generation is forty years. However, the dictionary definition of a generation is *the period of time between the birth of a male and the birth of his first child*, therefore, in Abraham's day a generation was *one hundred years*, because Abraham was one hundred years old when Isaac was born and the Bible tells us that Isaac, the child of promise, was Abraham's *only son* (Genesis 22:2, 22:12, 22:16). Calculating the length of a generation is important when first establishing the state of Israel in the territory God Almighty gave to the patriarchs and to their descendants; the importance will become clear as we proceed.

Bearing out the one hundred year generation in the last Scripture given above, which states that Abraham's offspring would be aliens in a land that is not theirs and oppressed for **four hundred years** but they would come back **in the fourth generation**, which again establishes our biblical one hundred-year generation.

Establishing a hundred-year generation in Abraham's day has tremendous bearing

Abraham, Isaac; and the everlasting covenant

today on God Almighty's covenant gift to Israel of all the land of Canaan for *"a thousand generations"* (Psalms 105:8). Elsewhere, God Almighty says Israel will inherit the land *"forever"* (Exodus 32:13). One thousand one hundred-year generations is one hundred thousand years, and from Abraham's day until this time of writing in 2021, Israel has only actually possessed the land for a little over four thousand and twenty years and the covenant still has almost ninety-six thousand years to run, which is why Almighty God described it as being "forever." This means that neither the antisemitic United Nations nor the antisemitic International Criminal Court will successfully limit Israel's use of her land.

Another thing to note is more serious. In one of the Scriptures above it states that Abraham's offspring would be oppressed for *four hundred years*, and the reason given for that length of oppression is that *"the iniquity of the Amorites is not yet complete."* This clearly indicates that God Almighty's patience waits for the sins of a particular nation to reach a certain level before He will justifiably bring terrible and existential judgements and destructions upon that nation. In the case of the Amorites God Almighty waited four hundred years before He moved against them when Israel came out of Egypt. It was necessary for the Israelites to suffer cruel slavery while the sin of the Amorites was growing to the point of no return. It was one of the first nations that fledgling Israel destroyed before it reached Canaan:—

> *I brought you to the land of the Amorites, who lived on the other side of the Jordan; they fought with you, and I handed them over to you, and you took possession of their land, and I destroyed them before you*
> (Joshua 24:8).

The Amorite lesson applies to every nation on earth, and nations today need to repent of their sins now, before the patience of God Almighty runs out. And it would be a mistake to think there is a set time limit before judgement falls. God Almighty gives clear warning to every nation:

> *See now that I, even I, am He; there is no God besides Me. I kill and I make alive; I wound and I heal; and no one can deliver from My hand.*
>
> *For I lift up my hand to heaven, and swear: As I live forever, when I whet my glittering sword, and My hand takes hold on judgment; I will take vengeance on all My adversaries, and will repay all those who hate Me*
> (Deuteronomy 32:39–41).

John Calvin, the French theologian, pastor and reformer in Geneva during the Protestant Reformation noted that disasters that afflict human existence, though punishments for the wicked, are an education for the believer; they strengthen faith, develop humility, purge wickedness, and compel him to keep alert and look to God for help.)

The ceremony for which Abraham was preparing the animals and birds was a standard procedure for all important covenants and contracts, including marriages. Entering into a covenant that included the cutting of animals in two signified to the parties walking between the pieces: "May it be so done to me and more so if I break the terms of this covenant." Anyone who considered breaking such a covenant knew that he immediately placed his life in great danger, as the following Scripture shows:—

And the men who transgressed My covenant and did not keep the terms of the covenant that they made before Me, I will make them like the calf that they cut in two and passed between its parts—the officials of Judah, the officials of Jerusalem, the eunuchs, the priests, and all the people of the land who passed between the parts of the calf. And I will give them into the hand of their enemies and into the hand of those who seek their lives. Their corpses will become food for the birds of the air and the wild animals of the earth (Jeremiah 34:18–19).

It was standard procedure for the parties of the covenant to walk between the parts of the slain animals, which was called "cutting a covenant," to say, "May it be so done to me and more so if I break the terms of this covenant," but the covenant that God Almighty was about to make with Abraham was different insofar as only God Almighty passed between the pieces of the animals, because it was God Almighty who was making the covenant, not Abraham, he was the recipient of the covenant. Therefore:—

> *When the sun had gone down and it was dark, a smoking fire pot and a flaming torch passed between these pieces. On that day the* L<small>ORD</small> *God Almighty made a covenant with Abraham, saying, "To your descendants I give this land, from the river of Egypt to the great river, the river Euphrates, the land of the Kenites, the Kenizzites, the Kadmonites, the Hittites, the Perizzites, the Rephaim, the Amorites, the Canaanites, the Girgashites, and the Jebusites"*
>
> (Genesis 15:17–21).

It is very important for the reader to understand the ramification of the covenant that God Almighty made with Abraham and his descendants that day. Appearing with fire and smoke, God Almighty *"swore with an oath"* to give the land to Abraham and his descendants (Ezekiel 20:28, 20:42, 47:14) as *an everlasting covenant* (Genesis 48:4), and in the covenant He set the boundaries of the future state of Israel that the descendants of Abraham would establish centuries later. The covenant cannot ever be rescinded, for as God Almighty passed between the pieces of the animals He said, "May it be so done to Me and more so if ever I break the terms of this covenant." The covenant God Almighty made with Abraham and his descendants concerning the land is an eternal covenant, as eternal as Day and Night.

Abraham, Isaac; and the everlasting covenant

Some ten or fifteen years had passed after Abraham's arrival in Canaan and he was still childless. At Sarah's suggestion he took Sarah's Egyptian maid, Hagar, as a concubine and had a son by her, whom he named Ishmael. Abraham was eighty-six years old when Hagar bore Ishmael.

About fourteen years later, Isaac—Abraham's son of God's promise—was born. As Isaac matured God Almighty appeared to him and reiterated the promise He had made to Abraham:—

Dwell in this land, and I will be with you and will bless you, for to you and to your offspring I will give all these lands, and I will establish the oath that I swore to Abraham your father. I will multiply your offspring as the stars of heaven and will give to your offspring all these lands. And in your offspring all the nations of the earth will be blessed, because Abraham obeyed my voice and kept my charge, my commandments, my statutes, and my laws (Genesis 26:3–5).

Isaac went on to marry Rebekah, his father's great niece and Isaac's cousin, and she bore him twin sons, Jacob and Esau. Jacob was a chronic conniver and his twin brother Esau, though he was the firstborn, despised his birthright and readily sold it to Jacob for a bowl of lentil soup and some bread when he came in from hunting and was hungry (Genesis 25:34). Later, with Rebekah's overt help—dressing Jacob in Esau's clothes to make him smell like Esau, and putting goat skins on his neck and hands to disguise his smooth skin and imitate Esau's hairy skin—Jacob swindled Esau out of his father's blessing for the firstborn—the double portion—and in that blessing Esau was made subservient to Jacob (Genesis 27:29). Isaac, whose eyes had set with age so that he could not see, was horrified to find that he had blessed Jacob with Esau's right of the firstborn's blessing, but said: *"I have blessed him—and indeed he will be blessed."* When Esau heard his father's words, he cried out with a loud and bitter cry, saying to his father, *"Bless me—me also father!"* But Isaac said, "Your brother came with deceit and has taken away your blessing." When Esau wanted to inherit the blessing, he forfeited it because *"he found no opportunity for repentance, although he sought the blessing with tears"* (Hebrews 12:17).

Esau vowed to kill Jacob because of his conniving (Genesis 27:41), but Jacob fled far away from Esau. He went to Haran in Mesopotamia to stay with an uncle, the brother of his mother.

Jacob

On his journey to Haran, because the sun had set, Jacob had to spend a night in the open. He lay down to sleep, with a rock for a pillow, and he dreamed. In his dream he saw a ladder set up on the earth, the top of it reached into heaven; and the angels of God Almighty were ascending and descending on it. And God Almighty stood above it and said to Jacob, "I am the LORD, the God of Abraham your father and the God of Isaac; the land on which you lie I will give to you and to your offspring." God Almighty also said to Jacob, "Know that I am with you and will keep you wherever you go, and will bring you back to this land; for I will not leave you until I have done what I have promised you." Then Jacob awoke from his sleep and said, "Surely the LORD is in this place—and I did not know it! It is none other than the house of God." Then Jacob took the stone that had served him as a pillow, set it up at his head place, and poured oil on it and called the place Bethel — (בית אל) — the house of God (Genesis 28:11–19).

(This was the first of many encounters that Jacob had with the LORD. Jacob began life as a conniver but was transformed into a devout and devoted servant of God Almighty, who expressed admiration for Jacob and greatly blessed him throughout his life. Jacob's genuine zeal for the LORD touched God's heart, inspiring the LORD to refer to Himself as *"the Holy One of Jacob"* (Isaiah 29:23) in contrast to *"the Holy One of Israel."* He also referred to Himself as *"the Mighty One of Jacob"* (Isaiah 60:16),

"the King of Jacob" (Isaiah 41:21), and
"the Portion of Jacob" (Jeremiah 10:16.)

In Haran, Jacob became indentured to his uncle Laban, Rebekah's brother, who made Jacob serve seven years for each of his two daughters, Rachel and Leah. Jacob greatly loved Rachel from the start and agreed to seven years of servitude for her, which seemed to pass like a few days because of his love for her, and when he had finished serving his term for Rachel he eagerly entered the tent that evening to consummate his marriage to her. However, in the morning Jacob found that it was Leah whom he had lain with that night and not Rachel. Jacob confronted the deceitful Laban and said, "Was it not for Rachel that I served you seven years, how could you deceive me so? Laban replied that it was not the custom to marry off the younger daughter before the firstborn. So Jacob fulfilled Leah's bridal week and then Laban gave his daughter Rachel to Jacob for another seven years of servitude, and Jacob loved Rachel more than Leah. Laban had also given his maid Zilpah to Leah as a maid, and also his maid Bilhah to Rachel as her maid.

Leah bore Jacob six sons and a daughter, Dinah. Rachel bore two sons to Jacob. Both maids were given to Jacob as concubines (recognized as wives with a lower social status) and both bore children to him, Bilhah bore two sons, which Rachel claimed as her own, and Zilpah also bore two sons to Jacob, which Leah claimed as her own.

Jacob fathered a total of thirteen children, twelve sons and one daughter. The twelve sons in order of birth, were: Reuben, Simeon, Levi, Judah, Dan, Naphtali, Gad,

Asher, Issachar, Zebulun, Joseph, and Benjamin. After completing his seven-year servitude for Rachel, Jacob said to Laban: —

Send me away, that I may go to my own home and country. Give me my wives and my children for whom I have served you, and let me go; for you know very well the service I have given you (Genesis 30:25–26).

But Laban did not want Jacob to leave and pressed him to stay, saying: *"Name me your wages, and I will give it"* (Genesis 30:28), to which Jacob replied: —

You know yourself how I have served you, and how your livestock has fared with me. For you had little before I came, and it has increased abundantly, and the LORD *has blessed you wherever I turned. But now when will I provide for my own household also?*
(Genesis 30:29–30).

Laban was insistent, and said, *"What wages will I give you?"* Jacob said to Laban:

You will not give me anything. Do this for me; I will again keep and feed your flock if you will let me pass through your flock today, removing every speckled and spotted sheep and every black lamb, and the spotted and speckled among the goats; and this will be my wages. So my honesty will answer for me later, when you come to look into my wages. Every one that is not speckled and spotted among the goats and black among the lambs, if found with me, will be counted as stolen. Laban said, "Good! Let it be just as you have said."

However, that day the crafty Laban removed the male goats that were striped and spotted, and all the female goats that were speckled and spotted, every one that had white on it, and every lamb that was black, and put them in the charge of his sons; and he set a distance of three days' journey between himself and Jacob, while Jacob was pasturing the rest of Laban's flock (Genesis 30:31–36).

Laban cheated on Jacob by first taking out of the flock what was rightfully going to be Jacob's wages before Jacob got to go through the flock himself. Then Laban put three days' journey between himself and Jacob in an attempt to prevent Jacob from finding out about his deceitful theft. The two master deceivers locked horns, but God Almighty is on Jacob's side and Laban proves to be no match for his God-inspired adversary and Laban's wealth ended up in Jacob's pocket:— *and female slaves, and camels and donkeys* (Genesis 30:37–42).

After many months God Almighty told Jacob to return to the land of his fathers, to his own kindred, so Jacob called Leah and Rachel to him in the fields and told them of his decision. He said to them:—

> *I see that your father does not regard me as favorably as he did before. But the God of my father has been with me. You know that I have served your father with all my strength; yet your father has cheated me and changed my wages ten times, but God did not permit him to harm me. If he said, 'The speckled will be your wages,' then all the flock bore speckled; and if he said, 'The striped will be your wages,' then all the flock bore striped.*
>
> *Jacob took fresh rods of poplar and almond and plane, and peeled white streaks in them, exposing the white of the rods. He set the rods that he had peeled in front of the flocks in the troughs, that is, the watering*

places, where the flocks came to drink. And since they bred when they came to drink, the flocks bred in front of the rods, and so the flocks produced young that were striped, speckled, and spotted. Jacob separated the lambs, and set the faces of the flocks toward the striped and the completely black animals in the flock of Laban; and he put his own droves apart, and did not put them with Laban's flock. Whenever the stronger of the flock were breeding, Jacob laid the rods in the troughs before the eyes of the flock, that they might breed among the rods, but for the feebler of the flock he did not lay them there; so the feebler were Laban's, and the stronger Jacob's. Thus the man grew exceedingly rich, and had large flocks, and male and female slaves, and camels and donkeys

(Genesis 30:37–42).

After many months God Almighty told Jacob to return to the land of his fathers, to his own kindred, so Jacob called Leah and Rachel to him in the fields and told them of his decision,

Rachel and Leah responded to Jacob and said:—

Is there any portion or inheritance left to us in our father's house? Are we not regarded by him as foreigners? For he has sold us, and he has been using up the money given for us. All the property that God has taken away from our father belongs to us and to our children; now then, do whatever God has said to you (Genesis 31:14–16).

Jacob arose and put his wives and children and their transportable possessions on camels, and drove all the livestock he had acquired before him to go to the land of Canaan, to his father Isaac.

Jacob deceived Laban by not informing him that he was going, and while Laban was away shearing his flock Rachel stole his household idols (gods). So Jacob fled with his family and all that he owned across the Euphrates River and headed for the hill country of Gilead. It was three days before Laban learned that Jacob had gone and Laban got his relatives together and pursued Jacob for seven days before overtaking him in Gilead.

Before Laban had caught up with Jacob God Almighty came to him in a dream of the night and said to him:— *"Take care that you say not a word to Jacob, either good or bad"* (Genesis 31:24). Jacob had encamped in the hill country of Gilead, and after Laban caught up with him he also made his camp there. Then Laban said to Jacob, "Why did you deceive me and carry away my daughters like captives taken with the sword? It is in my power to do you harm, but the God of your father spoke to me last night telling me, 'Be careful not to speak either good or bad to Jacob'. I can understand the longing for your father's house, but why did you steal my gods?"

Jacob answered and said, "I was afraid you would take your daughters by force. The one with whom you find your gods will not live in the presence of my kinsmen. Point out what is yours and take it for yourself" (Jacob did not know that Rachel had stolen Laban's gods). Laban searched Jacob's tent and Leah's tent and those of the two maids but did not find them. Laban then entered Rachel's tent and found her sitting on a camel's saddle (in which were her father's household idols). Rachel said to her father, "Please do not be angry that I cannot rise before you but the way of women (menstruation) is upon me." Laban searched the whole tent, but did not find them. Then Jacob got angry with Laban and said to him:—

What is my offense? What is my sin, that you have hotly pursued me? Although you have felt through all my goods, what have you found of all your household goods? Set it here before my kinsfolk and your kinsfolk, so that they may decide between us two. These twenty years I have been with you; your ewes and your female goats have not miscarried, and I have not eaten the rams of your flocks. That which was torn by wild beasts I did not bring to you; I bore the loss of it myself; of my hand you required it, whether stolen by day or stolen by night. It was like this with me: by day the heat consumed me, and the cold by night, and my sleep fled from my eyes. These twenty years I have been in your house; I served you fourteen years for your two daughters, and six years for your flock, and you have changed my wages ten times. If the God of my father, the God of Abraham and the Fear of Isaac, had not been on my side, surely now you would have sent me away empty-handed. God saw my affliction and the labor of my hands, and rebuked you last night
(Genesis 31:36–42).

Laban answered Jacob: —

The daughters are my daughters, the children are my children, the flocks are my flocks, and all that you see is mine. But what can I do today about these daughters of mine, or about their children whom they have borne? (Genesis 31:43).

Then Laban and Jacob made a covenant between themselves. Jacob set up a stone as a pillar and then they both piled stones into a heap and together they ate a meal and spent the night there. And Laban also said to Jacob: —

> *Here is this heap, and here is this pillar I have set up between you and me. This heap is a witness, and this pillar is a witness, that I will not go past this heap to your side to harm you and that you will not go past this heap and pillar to my side to harm me. May the God of Abraham and the God of Nahor, the God of their father, judge between us." So Jacob took an oath in the name of the Fear of his father Isaac*
>
> (Genesis 31:51–53).

Laban was apparently a polytheist, like his father Terah, who made idols for sale, which Abraham broke before leaving Haran. Laban swore an oath in the name of the God of Abraham and the name of the God of Nahor (another son of Terah), while Jacob swore the oath in the name of the God (Fear) of his father Isaac, the God whom Isaac worshiped with *awe* and with *trembling*.

> (It is interesting to note that ultra-Orthodox Jews today are called haredi Jews, and "hared" in Hebrew (חרד) means to tremble, therefore haredi Jews are Jews who purport to tremble before God.)

God's fighter

Laban returned home, while Jacob continued to head toward Canaan, the land of his family. As he went his way the angels of God met him, and when Jacob saw them he said, "This is God's camp!" So he called that place Mahanaim (מחנים) — *Two Camps* (Genesis 32:2).

Jacob had to give some thought to meeting his brother Esau, whom he had cheated both out of his birthright and of his father's special firstborn blessing. Jacob told some servants to go ahead of him to Esau in Edom and to inform him that he had been living with uncle Laban and had stayed until now. Jacob commanded his servants to tell Esau that he had oxen and camels, donkeys and flocks, male and female servants, and that he was sending some ahead so that he may find favor in Esau's sight.

Jacob's messengers returned saying, "We met with your brother Esau and he is coming to meet you, and he has four hundred men with him." At this Jacob became both afraid and deeply distressed. Pulling himself together he divided his people, his flocks and his herds into two companies, thinking that if Esau comes and attacks one company, then perhaps the other company could escape. Jacob then prayed to the God of Abraham and of his father Isaac and said: —

O God of my father Abraham and God of my father Isaac, O LORD who said to me, "Return to your country and to your kindred, and I will do you good," I am not worthy of the least of all the steadfast love and all the faithfulness that you have shown to your servant, for with only my staff I crossed this Jordan; and now I have become two companies. Deliver me, please, from the hand of my brother Esau, for I am afraid of

> him; he may come and kill us all, the mothers with the children. Yet you have said, "I will surely do you good, and make your offspring as the sand of the sea, which cannot be counted because of their number"
>
> (Genesis 32:9-13).

Jacob remained there that night and developed a plan to win Esau's favor. He began putting together a 'gift package' for his estranged brother: —

> *So from what he had he took a present for Esau, two hundred female goats and twenty male goats, two hundred ewes and twenty rams, thirty milk camels and their colts, forty cows, ten bulls, twenty female donkeys and ten male donkeys. These he delivered into the hands of his servants, every drove by itself, and he said to his servants, "Pass on ahead of me, and put a space between droves." He said to the leading servant, "When Esau my brother meets you, and asks, 'To whom do you belong? Where are you going? And whose are these ahead of you?' then you are to say, 'They belong to your servant Jacob; they are a gift for my lord Esau; and furthermore he is behind us.'" Jacob likewise instructed the second and the third servant and all who followed the droves, "You will say the same thing to Esau when you meet him, and you will say, 'Furthermore your servant Jacob is behind us.'" For Jacob thought, "I may appease him with the present that I am sending ahead of me, and afterwards I will see his face; perhaps he will accept me." So the present went on ahead of him; and he spent that night in the camp* (Genesis 32:13-21).

The night Jacob got up and took his wives, his concubines, and his children, and crossed the ford of the Jabbok. Jacob

God's fighter

took them and sent them across the stream, and also everything else that he had.

Jacob was left alone and a Man wrestled with him until daybreak. When the Man saw that he had not prevailed against Jacob he touched the socket of his thigh and dislocated it while He wrestled with him. The Man then said, "Let me go because the day is dawning," but Jacob said, "Not until you bless me."

> *So the Man said to him, "What is your name?" And he said, "Jacob." Then he said, "Your name shall no longer be called Jacob, but Israel, for you have struggled with God and with men, and have won." And he blessed Jacob there* (Genesis 32:27–28).

So Jacob named that place *Peniel* (פניאל), saying, "I have seen God Almighty face to face, and yet my life was spared." Jacob had indeed struggled with God and man and had prevailed. Jacob struggled with his brother even in Rebekah's womb (Genesis 25:22), and Jacob was born clutching Esau's heel (Genesis 25:26). Jacob struggled against Esau and prevailed over him when Esau sold his double portion birthright for a bowl of lentil stew and some bread (Genesis 25:29–34), and Jacob prevailed over both Esau and his father Isaac when he stole the birthright blessing. And Jacob prevailed against the Angel of the Lord, the visible manifestation of the invisible God, when Jacob refused to let Him go until He had blessed him.

The struggle with the visible manifestation of the invisible God was a watershed moment in the life of Jacob, who was now renamed to Israel (ישראל), meaning *"God's fighter,"* and it was a harbinger of the nation of Israel. As the sun rose that morning Jacob was limping on his thigh as he passed over Peniel. Even until today haredi Jews do not eat the sinew of the thigh that is on the hip socket, because the Angel of God touched the socket of Jacob's hip on the sinew of the thigh.

Another struggle faced Jacob; reconciling with his brother Esau twenty years after he had virtually stolen Esau's birthright—a double portion of all that his father had—and the blessing of the firstborn whereby Isaac had greatly blessed Jacob and had made Esau Jacob's servant. Jacob now had to face the consequences of his earlier actions and he was preparing for a worst-case scenario.

As he traveled toward Canaan Jacob looked up and saw his brother Esau coming, and four hundred men with him:—

So he divided the children among Leah and Rachel and the two maids. He put the maids with their children in front, then Leah with her children, and Rachel and Joseph last of all. He himself went on ahead of them, bowing himself to the ground seven times, until he came near his brother (Genesis 33:1–3).

Esau ran to meet Jacob and hugged and kissed him, and they both wept together. Then Esau saw the women and children who were with Jacob, and asked "Who are these with you?" Jacob told him that they were what God Almighty had graciously given to him. And the maids came with their children and they bowed down to Esau and then Leah came with her children and bowed down; and afterward Rachel came with Joseph, and they bowed down.

Then Esau said, "What is the meaning of all the droves I met earlier," and Jacob said they were to find favor in his eyes, but Esau said, "I have plenty, brother, keep what you have as your own," but Jacob said, "No, please, if I have found favor in your sight, then accept my gift from my hand for I see your face as one sees the face of God and you have received me favorably. So at Jacob's urging Esau accepted the gift.

Esau wanted to travel along with Jacob and his company, but Jacob said, "You know the children are young and frail, and the herds and flocks that are nursing are a concern for me, and if they are driven hard for even one day the flocks will die. Please go on ahead of me and I will follow at my leisure, according to the pace of the herds and the flocks and according to the pace of the children, until I come to you at Seir. So Esau began his return journey to Seir with his men that day.

Jacob traveled to Succoth where he built a house for himself and made shelters (סכת) for his livestock (Genesis 33:1–17). He then came to the city of Shechem, which is in the land of Canaan, and he camped in front of the city. And from the sons of Hamor, Shechem's father, Jacob bought the plot of land on which he had pitched his tent for one hundred pieces of silver. There he erected an altar and called it *El-Elohe-Israel* (אל אליה אשראל)—*The God of Israel is God*—(Genesis 33:18–20).

Now Dinah, the daughter whom Leah had borne to Jacob, went out to visit with her peers, the young women of the land. But Shechem, the son of Hamor the Hivite, who was the ruler of the region, took Dinah by force and lay with her. Shechem was smitten by Dinah, spoke tenderly to her, and asked his father to obtain Dinah for him as a wife. So Hamor went to talk with Jacob about it.

Jacob had heard about Shechem's rape of his daughter, but because his sons were out in the fields with the livestock he remained silent until they came in. After they came in and heard about the disgraceful thing that had been done to their sister, they were very angry.

Hamor spoke with them and said, "The soul of my son Shechem longs for your daughter, please give her in marriage to him: —

Make marriages with us; give your daughters to us, and take our daughters for your young men. You will live with us; and the land will be open to you; live and trade in it, and obtain property in it."

Shechem also said to Dinah's father and to her brothers, "Let me find favor with you, and whatever you say to me I will give. Put the bride price and gift I am to bring as high as you like, and I will give whatever you ask of me; only give me the girl to be my wife" (Genesis 34:9–12).

Jacob's sons answered Shechem and his father with deceit, because Shechem had defiled their sister Dinah by raping and humbling her. They said, "We cannot do this thing, to give our sister to one who is uncircumcised, for that would also be a disgraceful thing to us": —

On this one condition will we agree to you: that you become as we are and that every male among you be circumcised. Then we will give our daughters to you, and we will take your daughters for ourselves, and we will live among you and become one people. But if you do not agree to be circumcised, then we will take our sister and go (Genesis 34:15–17).

These words seemed reasonable to Hamor and Shechem, Hamor's son. The young man immediately got the plan into action, because he was smitten by Jacob's daughter, and he was the most admired in his father's family. So Hamor and Shechem went to the gate of the city and spoke to the men of the city, saying: —

These people are friendly with us; let them live in the land and trade in it, for the land is large enough for them; let us take their daughters in marriage, and let us give them our daughters. Only on this condition will they agree to live among us, to become one people: that every male among us be circumcised as they are circumcised. Will not their livestock, their property, and all their animals be ours? Only let us agree with them, and they will live among us." And all who went out of the city gate heeded Hamor and his son Shechem; and every male was circumcised, all who went out of the gate of his city

(Genesis 34:21–24).

On the third day following the circumcision, when the men were in great pain, Dinah's brothers, Simeon and Levy, took their swords and boldly came upon the unsuspecting city and slaughtered every male. They killed Hamor and his son Shechem and took Dinah from Shechem's house, and left. Then:—

The other sons of Jacob came upon the slain and pillaged them and the city, because they had defiled their sister. They took their flocks and their herds, their donkeys, and whatever was in the city and in the field. All their wealth, all their little ones and their wives, all that was in the houses, they captured and pillaged (Genesis 34:27–29).

(If there is one word or action that summarises the lives of those who lived before and after Abraham and Isaac in our story, it would be deceit. Such crudely performed circumcisions with flint knives would have incapacitated the Shechemite men, especially after two or three days when the inflammation would have been at its height and accompanied by fever; they would have been really helpless. The wholesale slaughter of all the men, the plunder of the city and abduction of all the women for the sin of one man is almost beyond belief.

Deceit is a typically middle-eastern trait, which still runs in the blood of those living in that region today. The trait is in the DNA of all the fathers, their wives, their sons, their daughters, their aunts and their uncles; little has changed since the days of Jacob, Rebekah, Laban, Leah and Rachel. Adding to this potent brew was Abraham, who *"listened to the voice of Sarai"* his wife (Genesis 16:2), and fathered *Ishmael* through Hagar, Sarai's Egyptian maid (Genesis 16:15). And of Ishmael the LORD God prophesied: —

He will be a wild donkey of a man; his hand will be against everyone and everyone's hand will be against him, and he will live in hostility toward all his brothers (Genesis 16:12)

Thus we have a very volatile mix — Arabs and Jews — living together in the same region today, which is why the Middle East is justifiably termed a powder keg. Camels, donkeys and swords have been replaced by Merkava battle tanks, Surface to Surface missiles, and Uzi machine guns.

The region known as the Middle East today has been previously conquered and reconquered by every superpower in the West. This has created a region rich in a culture of resistance and thousands of ethnic groups looking for their piece of land. This has created a complicated region in which powerful old predatory empires seek to rebuild themselves today. The numbers of past wars have been more than in any other region of the world, and the numbers of airstrikes and battles taking place in the Middle East today make it the most war-torn region in the world and with the largest number of protagonists. But we are getting ahead of the story. We must needs return to the lives of Jacob and his progeny.)

Jacob becomes Israel

After Jacob's sons, Simeon and Levi, slaughtered all the males of the city of Shechem, and his other sons looted the city of all its goods and livestock, and its women and children, Jacob said to them, "You have made me odious among the Canaanites and they may gather together against me and destroy me and my household, who are only a few compared to them," but his sons—Dinah's brothers—said to him, "Should he treat our sister like a prostitute?" (Genesis 34:30–31). Then God Almighty said to Jacob, "Go up to Bethel and live there, and make an altar there to the LORD God who appeared to you when you fled from your brother Esau." So Jacob said to all who were with him, "Come, let us go up to Bethel and I will make an altar there to God who answered me in the day of my distress and who has been with me wherever I have gone" (Genesis 35:3). Jacob first made his people surrender to him all their idols and gods, their earrings, amulets and charms, and he buried them beneath a great oak tree. Jacob was determined that only God Almighty was to be worshiped and followed by his people.

As they traveled there was great terror upon the people of the cities around them, and they did not pursue Jacob and his sons. And so Jacob and all who were with him came to Bethel, which is in the land of Canaan, and he built an altar there as the LORD God had commanded him. He called the place *El Bethel* (אל ביתאל)—*God of the house of God*—because there God Almighty had revealed Himself to him when he fled from his brother Esau (Genesis 35:7). Then God Almighty appeared to Jacob again and He blessed him and said to him:—

Your name is Jacob; no longer will you be called Jacob, but Israel will be your name." So He renamed him Israel (Genesis 35:10).

Then the LORD God said to Israel:—

I am God Almighty: be fruitful and multiply; a nation and a company of nations will come from you, and kings will come forth from you. The land that I gave to Abraham and Isaac I will give to you, and I will also give the land to your offspring after you
(Genesis 35:11–12)

Then God Almighty went up from Israel at the place where He had spoken with him, and Israel set up a pillar there, a pillar of stone, and he poured out a drink offering on it, and also poured oil on it. So Israel called the place where God had spoken with him *Bethel* (ביתאל)—*The house of God*—(Genesis 35:15).

They all journeyed onward from Bethel and while they were still some distance from Ephrath (Bethlehem), Rachel began to give birth and suffered severe labor. As Rachel was in hard labor the midwife said to her, "Do not despair, you have another son." And it happened that as her soul was departing (for she died), she named the boy Ben-Oni—*"son of my sorrow"*—but Israel called him Benjamin—*"son of my right hand."* So Rachel died there and was buried on the way to Ephrath, which is Bethlehem (Genesis 35:16–19). So Israel set up a pillar over her grave and Rachel's monument is there to this day.

Israel traveled on and pitched his tent beyond the tower of Eder. While Israel was living in that region, Reuben, Israel's firstborn, went in and lay with Israel's concubine Bilhah—formerly Rachel's maid—who was the mother of

Jacob becomes Israel

Dan and Naphtali, and Israel heard about it. Reuben's sin was to cost him his birthright:—

The sons of Reuben the firstborn of Israel. (He was the firstborn, but because he defiled his father's bed his birthright was given to the sons of Joseph, the son of Israel, so that Reuben is not enrolled in the genealogy according to the birthright

(1Chronicles 5:1).

Eventually, Israel returned to his father Isaac in Mamre, to Kiriath Arba (Hebron), where Abraham and Isaac had stayed (Genesis 35:27). Isaac lived one hundred and eighty years before he died. He was gathered to his ancestors, old and full of days; and Esau and Jacob buried him. Israel then continued to live in the land of Canaan where his father Isaac had lived.

Joseph

Israel loved Joseph more than any of his other children, because he *was* the son of his old age. Israel also made him a special tunic, a long-sleeved ornate coat of many colors (Genesis 37:3). When his brothers saw that their father paid more attention to him than to all his brothers, they hated him and would not speak amicably to him.

At a time when Joseph was seventeen he was caring for the flocks with his brothers, the sons of Bilhah and Zilpah, his father's wives (concubines), and he brought his father a bad report about them. Then one day Joseph had a dream, and when he told it to his brothers, they hated him even more. He said to them, "Listen to this dream. There we were, binding sheaves in the field, when suddenly my sheaf rose up and stood upright; then your sheaves gathered around and bowed down to it." His brothers said to him, "Are you really going to reign over us? Are you going to have domination over us?" After that they hated him yet still more because of his dreams (Genesis 37:5–8).

Joseph later had a second dream, and told it to his brothers, saying, "Look, I have had another dream: the sun, the moon, and eleven stars were bowing down to me." But when he told it to his father Israel and to his brothers, Israel rebuked him, and said to him, "What kind of dream is this that you have had? Will I and your mother and your brothers, come and bow down before you?" His brothers were jealous of him, but Israel kept the matter of the dreams in mind (Genesis 37:9–11).

Joseph's brothers went to pasture their father's flock near Shechem. Israel said to Joseph, "Are not your brothers pasturing the flock at Shechem? Come, I will send you to them." So Israel said to Joseph, "Go and see if it is well with your brothers and with the flock and bring me word." Joseph had trouble finding his brothers and kept walking until he eventually found them at Dothan.

Joseph's brothers saw him from a distance and, before he got near them, conspired to kill him. They spoke to one another saying, "Here comes the dreamer. Let us kill him and throw him into one of the pits and then we can say that a wild animal has devoured him; then we will see what becomes of his dreams." However, when Reuben heard of it, he rescued Joseph out of their hands by saying, "Let us not take his life. Shed no blood; throw him into this pit in the wilderness, but do not lay a hand on him." Reuben thought he could rescue Joseph out of their hands and restore him to his father. So when Joseph came up to his brothers they stripped him of his long-sleeved robe of many colors and threw him into a cistern that had no water in it (Genesis 37:18–24).

Then the brothers sat down to eat; and looking up they saw a caravan of Ishmaelites (Arabs) coming from Gilead, with their camels carrying gum, balm, and resin, taking it down to Egypt. Then Judah said, "What does it profit us if we kill our brother and cover up his blood? Come, let us sell him to the Ishmaelites, and not lay our hands on him, for he is our brother, our own flesh." At this his brothers agreed.

So when the Arab merchants passed by, Joseph's brothers pulled him out of the cistern and sold him to the Ishmaelites for twenty pieces of silver. The Ishmaelites then took Joseph to Egypt (Genesis 37:28).

When Reuben returned to the cistern and saw that Joseph was not in it, he tore his clothes, and, returning to his brothers he said, "The boy is gone; and I, how can I account for this?" Then they took Joseph's robe, killed a goat, and dipped the robe in the blood. Then they took the long robe with sleeves to their father, and they said, "We have found this; see whether it is your son's robe or not." Israel recognized it, and said, "It is my son's robe! A wild animal has devoured him; Joseph is without doubt torn to pieces." Then Israel tore his garments and put sackcloth around his waist and mourned for Joseph many days. All Israel's sons and all his daughters (in law) sought to comfort him; but he refused to be comforted and said, "I will go down to the grave, to my son, mourning." And so Joseph's father wept for him. Meanwhile the Ishmaelites had sold Joseph in Egypt, to Potiphar, the captain of Pharaoh's guard (Genesis 37:29–36).

> (All of the events portrayed here were predetermined by God Almighty. They are part and parcel of His divine plan for His people Israel. Joseph's dream of his brothers bowing down to him, and the dream where his father and mother also bowed down to him, showed the unmistakable supremacy of Joseph, first over his brothers, and then over the whole house of Israel. The repetition shows the certainty of the dreams coming to pass.)

Joseph in Egypt

God Almighty was with Joseph in Egypt. Potiphar, the Egyptian chief officer of Pharaoh's guard, bought him from the Arabs who had brought him to Egypt. Joseph lived in his master's house and became successful and found favor in his master's eyes. Potiphar saw that the LORD God made everything prosper under Joseph's hand and he made him overseer over his house, and over all that he owned. The LORD's blessing was upon the Egyptian's house because of Joseph, upon his house and upon his fields. So Potiphar's only concern was with the food that he ate.

After a time Potiphar's wife looked with desire upon Joseph, for he was very handsome in face and form. One day she said to Joseph, "Come lie with me." He refused and said to his master's wife, "With me here my master concerns himself with nothing in the house, and he has put everything he owns into my hand. No one is greater in this house than I, and he has not kept back anything from me except yourself, because you are his wife. How then could I do such a great wickedness, and sin against God Almighty?" And though she spoke to Joseph day after day, he refused to go to bed with her or even be with her (Genesis 39:7–10). However:—

> *One day when he went into the house to do his work, and while no one else was in the house, she caught hold of his garment, saying, "Lie with me!" But he left his garment in her hand and fled outside. When she saw that he had left his garment in her hand and had fled outside, she called out to the members of her household and said to them, "See, my husband has*

brought a Hebrew among us to insult us! He came in to me to lie with me, and I cried out with a loud voice; and when he heard me raise my voice and cry out, he left his garment beside me, and ran outside." Then she kept his garment by her until his master came home, and she told him the same story, saying, "The Hebrew servant, whom you have brought among us, came in to me to insult me; but as soon as I raised my voice and cried out, he left his garment beside me, and fled outside" (Genesis 39:11–19).

When Potiphar heard his wife saying, "This is how your slave treated me," he was furious and burned with anger. So Potiphar took Joseph and put him in the prison where Pharaoh's prisoners were confined, and there Joseph was: in jail. However, God Almighty was with Joseph and showed kindness to him, giving him favor in the eyes of the chief jailer who committed all the prisoners into Joseph's care, so that Joseph was responsible for everything done in the prison. The chief jailer paid no attention to anything that was in Joseph's care, because the LORD God was with him; and whatever he did, the LORD made it prosper (Genesis 39:19–23).

In time it came about that both Pharaoh's cupbearer and also his baker offended him. Pharaoh was angry with the two officers, the chief cupbearer and the chief baker, and he put them in custody in the house of the captain of the guard, in the prison where Joseph was confined. The captain of the guard assigned Joseph to them, and he waited on them; and they were held in custody for some length of time (Genesis 40:1–4).

One night they both dreamed—the cupbearer and the baker of Pharaoh, who were both confined in the prison—

each dreamed a dream, each with its own interpretation. When Joseph came to them in the morning he saw that they were troubled, so he asked Pharaoh's officers, "Why are your faces so sad?" They said to him, "We have both had dreams, and there is no one to interpret them." Joseph said to them, "Do not interpretations belong to God Almighty? Please tell your dreams to me" (Genesis 40:5–8).

> So the chief cupbearer told his dream to Joseph and said to him, "In my dream there was a vine before me, and on the vine there were three branches. As soon as it budded, its blossoms shot forth, and the clusters ripened into grapes. Pharaoh's cup was in my hand, and I took the grapes and pressed them into Pharaoh's cup and placed the cup in Pharaoh's hand." Then Joseph said to him, "This is its interpretation: the three branches are three days. In three days Pharaoh will lift up your head and restore you to your office, and you will place Pharaoh's cup in his hand as formerly, when you were his cupbearer. Only remember me, when it is well with you, and please do me the kindness to mention me to Pharaoh, and so get me out of this house. For I was indeed stolen out of the land of the Hebrews, and here also I have done nothing that they should put me into this dungeon"
> (Genesis 40:9–15).

When the chief baker saw that the interpretation was favorable, he said to Joseph:—

> I also had a dream: there were three cake baskets on my head, and in the top basket there were all sorts of baked food for Pharaoh, but the birds were eating it out of the basket." And Joseph answered, "This is

its interpretation: the three baskets are three days; within three days Pharaoh will lift up your head—from you!—and hang you on a pole; and the birds will eat the flesh from you."

On the third day, which was Pharaoh's birthday, he made a feast for all his servants, and lifted up the head of the chief cupbearer and the head of the chief baker among his servants. He restored the chief cupbearer to his cupbearing, and he placed the cup in Pharaoh's hand; but the chief baker he hanged, just as Joseph had interpreted to them. Yet the chief cupbearer did not remember Joseph, but forgot him
(Genesis 40:16–23).

After two more years had passed, Pharaoh dreamed a dream. In the dream he was standing by the Nile and there came up out of the Nile seven sleek, fat cows, and they grazed in the reed grass. Then seven other cows, thin and ugly, came up out of the Nile after them, and they stood by the other cows on the bank of the Nile. Then the ugly and thin cows ate up the seven sleek, fat cows. Then Pharaoh awoke. He fell asleep again and dreamed a second time; seven ears of grain, plump and good, were growing on one stalk. Then seven ears, thin and blighted by the east wind, sprouted after them. The thin ears swallowed up the seven plump and full ears. Pharaoh awoke, and it was a dream. In the morning his spirit was troubled; so he sent and called for all the magicians of Egypt and all its wise men. Pharaoh told them his dreams, but there was no one who could interpret them for him (Genesis 41:1–8).

The chief cupbearer said to Pharaoh, "I remember my faults today. Once, Pharaoh was angry with his servants, and put me and the chief baker in custody in the house of the captain of the guard. We both dreamed a dream on the same night, he and I, each with its own meaning. A young Hebrew man was there with us, a servant of the captain of the guard. When we told him, he interpreted our dreams to us, giving an interpretation to each according to his dream. As he interpreted to us, so it turned out; I was restored to my office, and the baker was hanged" (Genesis 41:9–13).

Then Pharaoh sent for Joseph, and he was hurriedly brought out of the dungeon. When he had shaved and changed his clothes, he came in before Pharaoh, and Pharaoh said to Joseph:—

I have had a dream, and there is no one who can interpret it. I have heard it said of you that when you hear a dream you can interpret it. Joseph answered Pharaoh, "It is not in me; God Almighty will give Pharaoh a favorable answer." Then Pharaoh said to Joseph, "In my dream I was standing on the banks of the Nile; and seven cows, fat and sleek, came up out of the Nile and fed in the reed grass. Then seven other cows came up after them, poor, very ugly, and thin. Never had I seen such ugly ones in all the land of Egypt. The thin and ugly cows ate up the first seven fat cows, but when they had eaten them no one would have known that they had done so, for they were still as ugly and as thin as before. Then I awoke. I fell asleep a second time and I saw in my dream seven ears of grain, full and good, growing on one stalk, and seven ears, withered, thin, and blighted by the east wind, sprouting after them; and the thin ears swallowed up the seven good ears. But when I told it to the magicians no one could explain it to me"

(Genesis 41:14–24).

Then Joseph said to Pharaoh, "Pharaoh's dreams are one and the same; God Almighty has shown Pharaoh what He is about to do":—

The seven good cows are seven years, and the seven good ears are seven years; the dreams are one. The seven lean and ugly cows that came up after them are seven years, as are the seven empty ears blighted by the east wind. They are seven years of famine. It is as I told Pharaoh; Almighty God has shown Pharaoh what he is about to do. There will come seven years of great plenty throughout all the land of Egypt. After them there will arise seven years of famine, and all the plenty will be forgotten in the land of Egypt; the famine will consume the land. The plenty will no longer be known in the land because of the famine that will follow, for it will be very grievous. And the doubling of Pharaoh's dream means that the thing is fixed by God, and God will shortly bring it about. Now therefore, let Pharaoh select a man who is discerning and wise, and set him over the land of Egypt. Let Pharaoh proceed to appoint overseers over the land, and take one-fifth of the produce of the land of Egypt during the seven plentiful years. Let them gather all the food of these good years that are coming, and lay up grain under the authority of Pharaoh for food in the cities, and let them keep it. That food will be a reserve for the land against the seven years of famine that are to befall the land of Egypt, so that the land may not perish through the famine

(Genesis 41:25–36).

Joseph's advice pleased Pharaoh and all his officials. Pharaoh said to them, "Can we find a man like this—one in whom is the spirit of God?" So Pharaoh said to Joseph:—

Since God has shown you all this, there is no one so discerning and wise as you. You will be over my house, and all my people will order themselves as you command; only with regard to the throne will I be greater than you. And Pharaoh said to Joseph, "See, I have set you over all the land of Egypt." Removing his signet ring from his hand, Pharaoh put it on Joseph's hand; he arrayed him in garments of fine linen, and put a gold chain around his neck. He had him ride in the chariot of his second-in-command; and they cried out in front of him, "Bow the knee!"
(Genesis 41:37–43).

Consequently Pharaoh set Joseph over all the land of Egypt. In addition, Pharaoh said to Joseph, "I am Pharaoh, and without your consent no one will lift up hand or foot in all the land of Egypt." Pharaoh gave Joseph the name Zaphenath-paneah—*sustainer of life*; and he gave him Asenath daughter of Potiphera, priest of On, as his wife. Thus Joseph gained authority over the land of Egypt (Genesis 41:43–45).

Joseph and his brothers

Joseph was thirty years old when he entered into the service of Pharaoh, the king of Egypt. Joseph went out from the presence of Pharaoh and traveled throughout all Egypt, familiarizing himself with the land. During the seven good years the earth produced copiously. Joseph gathered up all the excess produce of the bountiful seven years when there was plenty in the land of Egypt, and stored up food in the cities; he stored up in every city the food from the fields round about it. So Joseph stored up excess grain in such abundance—like the sand of the sea—that he stopped measuring it, because it was so beyond human measure (Genesis 41:46–49).

Before the years of famine came, Joseph had two sons, whom Asenath bore to him. Joseph named the firstborn Manasseh—*causing to forget*—"For," he said, "God has made me forget all my hardship and all my father's house." The second he named Ephraim—*double-fruitfulness*—"For God has made me fruitful in the land of my misfortunes" (Genesis 41:50–52).

The seven years of plenty that had prevailed in the land of Egypt came to an end; and the seven years of famine began, just as Joseph had foretold. There was famine in every country round about, but throughout the land of Egypt there was bread. When all the land of Egypt was famished, the people cried to Pharaoh for bread and Pharaoh said to the Egyptians, "Go to Joseph and do what he says to you." The famine had spread over all the land, so Joseph opened the storehouses and sold to the Egyptians, for the famine was severe in Egypt. People from all the world also came to Egypt to buy grain, because the famine was severe throughout the world (Genesis 41:53–57).

Israel learned there was grain in Egypt and said to his sons, "Why do you keep looking at one another? I have heard that there is grain in Egypt; go down and buy grain for us there, that we may live and not die." So ten of Joseph's brothers went down to Egypt to buy grain, but Israel did not send Joseph's brother Benjamin, because he feared harm might come to him. So the sons of Israel were among the other people who came to buy grain, for the famine was acute in the land of Canaan (Genesis 42:1–5).

Joseph was now governor over all Egypt and it was he who sold grain to the people. Given time, Joseph's brothers came and bowed before him with their faces to the ground. Joseph recognized his brothers when he saw them, but he treated them like strangers and spoke roughly to them. "Where do you come from?" he asked, and they said, "From the land of Canaan, we came to to buy food." Joseph recognized his brothers, but they did not recognize him, and he recalled the dreams that he had dreamed about them.

Joseph said to them, "You are spies; you have come to see the nakedness of the land!" His brothers replied, "No, my lord; your servants have come to buy food. We are all sons of one man; we are honest men; your servants have never been spies." However, he continued to accuse them, saying, "No, you have come to see the nakedness of the land!" They said, "We, your servants, are twelve brothers, the sons of one man in the land of Canaan; the youngest, however, is now with our father, and one is no more."

Joseph said to them, "It is just as I have said; you are spies! Here is how you will be tested: as Pharaoh lives, you will not leave this place unless your youngest brother comes here! Let one of you go and bring your brother, while the rest of you remain in prison, in order that your words may be tested, whether there is truth in what you say; or else, as Pharaoh lives, surely you are spies." And he put them all together in prison for three days (Genesis 42:6–17).

> (At this point the ten brothers must have been beginning to contemplate the Scripture:— *"you may be sure that your sin will find you out"* (Numbers 32:23), over the wickedness they perpetrated against their brother Joseph years earlier. And Joseph was tasting the sweetness of revenge against his brothers for the harm they had collectively done to him; a revenge that he would later magnify.)

On their third day in prison Joseph said to them, "Do this and you will live, for I fear God: if you are honest men, let one of your brothers remain imprisoned here while the rest of you go and carry grain for the famine of your households, and then bring your youngest brother to me. With this your words will be verified and you will not die." The brothers agreed to Joseph's terms.

They said to one another, "We are paying the penalty for what we did to our brother; we saw his fear when he pleaded with us, but we would not listen. That is why this anguish has come upon us." Then Reuben said, "Did I not tell you not to wrong the lad? But you would not listen. So now there comes a reckoning for his blood."

They did not know that Joseph understood them, since he spoke with them through an interpreter. He went away from them and wept; then he returned and spoke to them. He picked out Simeon and had him bound in their presence. Joseph then gave orders to fill their bags with grain, to return every man's money to his sack, and to give them provisions for their journey back. All this was done for them.

The nine brothers loaded their donkeys with their grain, and departed. When one of them opened his sack at the lodging place to give his donkey some fodder, he saw his money at the top of the sack. He said to his brothers, "My money has been put back; here it is in my sack!" At this their hearts fell and they turned trembling to one another, saying, "What is this that God has done to us?" (Genesis 42:18–28).

When they came to their father Israel in the land of Canaan, they told him all that had happened to them, saying: —

The man, the lord of the land, spoke harshly to us, and charged us with spying on the land. But we said to him, "We are honest men, we are not spies. We are twelve brothers, sons of our father; one is no more, and the youngest is now with our father in the land of Canaan." Then the man, the lord of the land, said to us, 'By this I will know that you are honest men: leave one of your brothers with me, take grain for the famine of your households, and go your way. Bring your youngest brother to me, and I will know that you are not spies but honest men. Then I will release your brother to you, and you may trade in the land'"

(Genesis 42:29–34).

As they were emptying their sacks of grain at home, they found, in each one's sack, his bag of money. When they and their father saw their bundles of money, they were dismayed. Their father Israel said to them, "I am the one you have bereaved of children: Joseph is no more, and Simeon is no more, and now you would take Benjamin away from me!"

Then Reuben said to his father, "You can kill my two sons if I do not bring him back to you. Put him in my hands, and I will bring him back to you." But Israel said, "Benjamin will not go down with you, for his brother is dead and he alone is left of his mother's children. If any harm comes to him on the journey that you are to make, you would bring down my gray hairs with sorrow to Sheol (the abode of the dead)" (Genesis 42:35–38).

The famine was extremely severe in Canaan, and when Israel's family had eaten up the grain they had brought from Egypt, their father said to them, "Go again, buy us a little more food." However, Judah said to him, "The man unmistakably warned us, saying, 'You will not see my face unless your brother is with you.' If you will send Benjamin with us, we will go down and buy you food; but if you will not send him, we will not go down, for the man said to us, 'You will not see my face, unless your brother is with you.'"

Israel said, "Why did you treat me so badly as to tell the man that you had another brother?" They replied, "The man carefully questioned us about ourselves and our family, saying, 'Is your father still alive? Have you another brother?' What we told him was in answer to his questions. Could we in any way know that he would say, 'Bring your brother down'?" Then Judah said to his father, "Send Benjamin with me, and let us be on our way, so that we may all live and not die—you and we and also our little ones. I myself will be surety for him; you can hold me accountable for him. If I do not bring him back to you and set him before you, then let me bear the blame forever. If we had not delayed, we would now have returned twice" (Genesis 43:1–10).

> *Then their father Israel said to them, "If it must be so, then do this: take some of the choice fruits of the land in your bags, and carry them down as a present to the man—a little balm and a little honey, gum, resin, pistachio nuts, and almonds. Take double the money with you. Carry back with you the money that was returned in the top of your sacks; perhaps it was an oversight. Take your brother also, and be on your way again to the man; may God Almighty grant you mercy before the man, so that he may send back Benjamin and your other brother. As for me, if I am bereaved of my children, I am bereaved"*
>
> (Genesis 43:11–14).

So the brothers took the present, and they took double the money with them, as well as their brother Benjamin. Then they went on their way down to Egypt, and stood before Joseph (Genesis 43:15).

Now when Joseph saw his brother Benjamin with them, he said to the steward of his house, "Bring the men into the house, slaughter an animal and make ready, for these men are to eat with me at noon." The man did as Joseph commanded, and brought the brothers to Joseph's house. Now the brothers were afraid because they were brought to Joseph's house, and they said, "It is because of the money that was replaced in our sacks the first time, that he may have an opportunity to fall upon us, to make slaves of us and take our donkeys." So they went to Joseph's steward and spoke with him at the entrance to the house. They said, "Oh, my lord, we came down the first time to buy food; and when we came to the lodging place we opened our sacks, and there was each one's money in the top of his sack, our money was there in full, so we have brought it back. Moreover we have brought additional money with us to buy food. We do not know who put our money in our sacks." The steward replied, "Rest assured, do not be afraid; your God and the God of your father must have put treasure in your sacks for you; I received your money." Then he brought Simeon out to them. When the steward had brought the men into Joseph's house, and given them water, and they had washed their feet, and after he had given their donkeys food, they made the present ready for Joseph's coming at noon, for they had heard that they would be eating there (Genesis 43:16–25).

When Joseph came home, the brothers gave him the present that they had brought into the house, and bowed before him. He inquired about their welfare, and said, "Is your father well, the old man of whom you spoke? Is he still alive?" They said, "Your servant our father is well; he is still alive." They bowed their heads and paid respect to Joseph. Then he looked up and saw his brother Benjamin, his mother's son, and said, "Is this your youngest brother, of whom you spoke? God be gracious to you, my son!"

With that, Joseph hurried out, because he was overcome with emotion and affection for his brother, and he was about to shed tears. So he went into a private room and wept there. Then he washed his face and came out; and controlling himself he said, "Serve the meal." They served him by himself, and the eleven brothers by themselves, and the Egyptians who ate with him by themselves, because the Egyptians could not eat with the Hebrews, for that would be an abomination to the Egyptians. When they were seated before him, the firstborn according to his birthright and the youngest according to his youth, the brothers looked at one another in amazement. Portions were taken to them from Joseph's table, but Benjamin's portion was five times as much as any of theirs. So they drank and were merry with him (Genesis 43:26–34).

That evening Joseph commanded the steward of his house, "Fill the men's sacks with food, as much as they can carry, and put each man's money in the top of his sack. Also put my silver cup in the top of the sack of the youngest, with his money for the grain." And he did as Joseph had told him. As soon as there was sufficient morning light the brothers were sent away with their donkeys. When they had only gone a short distance from the city, Joseph said to his steward: —

> *Go, follow after the men; and when you overtake them, say to them, "Why have you returned evil for good? Why have you stolen my silver cup? Is it not from this that my lord drinks? Does he not indeed use it for divination? You have done wrong in doing this"*
>
> (Genesis 44:1–5).

When Joseph's steward overtook them, he repeated Joseph's words to them. They said to him, "Why does my lord speak such words as these? Far be it from us that we should do such a thing! Look, the money that we found at the top of our sacks, we brought back to you from the land of Canaan; why then would we steal silver or gold from your lord's house? Should it be found with any one of your servants, let him die; moreover the rest of us will become my lord's slaves."

Joseph's steward said, "In accordance with your words, let it be so. He with whom it is found will become

Joseph and his brothers

my slave, but the rest of you will go free." Then each one quickly lowered his sack to the ground and opened his sack. He searched, beginning with the eldest and ending with the youngest; and the cup was found in Benjamin's sack. At this they tore their clothes. Then each one loaded his donkey, and they returned to the city (Genesis 44:6–13).

Judah and his brothers came to Joseph's house while he was still there; and they dropped to the ground before him. Joseph said to them, "What deed is this that you have done? Do you not know that one such as I can practice divination?"

> (Joseph did not practice divination, but could have; with his ultra-high office in the land of Egypt it would have been normal had he done so. Placing the cup in Benjamin's sack was a strategic move by Joseph; it produced all the required results. His brothers' earlier cruel act against him was revealed to all and the accusations and threats by Joseph's steward had instilled fear into their hearts.)

Then Judah said, "What can we say to my lord? What can we speak? How can we clear ourselves? Almighty God has exposed our guilt; here we are then, my lord's slaves, both we and also the one in whose possession the cup has been found." Joseph's Steward said, "Far be it from me that I should do so! Only the one in whose possession the cup was found will be my slave; but as for you, go up in peace to your father" (Genesis 44:14–17).

Then Judah went up to Joseph and said, "O my lord, let me please speak a word to you and do not be angry with me; for you are like Pharaoh himself. My lord asked us, saying, 'Have you a father or a brother?' And we said, 'We have a father, an old man, and a young brother, the child of his father's old age. His brother is dead; and he alone is left of his mother's children, and our father loves him.' Then you said to us, 'Bring him down to me, so that I can see him.' We said to my lord, 'The boy cannot leave his father, for if he should leave his father, his father would die.' Then you said to your servants, 'Unless your youngest brother comes with you, you will see my face no more.' When we went back to my father we told him your words. So, when our father said, 'Go again, buy us a little food,' we said, 'We cannot go down. Only if Benjamin goes with us, will we go down; for we cannot see the man's face unless our young brother is with us.' Then my father said to us, 'You know that my wife bore me two sons; one left me, and I said, Surely he has been torn to pieces; and I have never seen him since. If you take this one from me also, and harm comes to him, you will bring down my gray hairs in sorrow to Sheol (the place of the dead).' Therefore, when I come to my father and Benjamin is not with us, then, as his life is bound up in the boy's life, when he sees that the boy is not with us, he will die; and we will bring down the gray hairs of our father with sorrow to the grave. For your servant became surety for the boy to my father, saying, 'If I do not bring him back to you, then I will bear the blame in the sight of my father all my life.' Now, please let me remain as a slave to my lord in place of the boy; and let the boy go back with his brothers. For how can I go back to my father if the boy is not with me? I fear to see the suffering that would come upon my father" (Genesis 44:18–34).

Joseph could no longer control himself before all those who stood by him, and he cried out, "Send everyone away from me." So no one stayed with him when Joseph made himself known to his brothers. And Joseph wept so loudly that the Egyptians heard it, and the household of Pharaoh heard it. Joseph said to his brothers, "I am Joseph. Is my father still alive?" But his brothers could not answer him, because they were distressed in his presence.

Then Joseph said to his brothers, "Come closer to me." And they came closer. He said, "I am your brother, Joseph, whom you sold into Egypt. Now, do not be distressed or angry with yourselves, because you sold me to those who brought me here; for God sent me before you to preserve life. For the famine has been in the land these past two years; and there are five more years in which there will be neither plowing nor harvest. God Almighty sent me before you to preserve for you a remnant on earth, and to keep alive many survivors. So it was not you who sent me here, but God Almighty; He has made me a father to Pharaoh, and lord of all his house and ruler over all the land of Egypt. Hurry and go up to my father and say to him, 'Thus says your son Joseph, God Almighty has made me lord of all Egypt; come down to me, do not delay. You will settle in the land of Goshen, and you will be near me, you and your children and your children's children, as well as your flocks, your herds, and all that you have. I will provide for you there—since there are five more years of famine to come—so that you and your household, and all that you have, will not come to poverty.' Now your eyes and the eyes of my brother Benjamin see that it is my own lips that speak to you. You must tell my father how greatly honored I am in Egypt, and all that you have seen. Hurry and bring my father down here." Then he fell upon his brother Benjamin's neck and wept, while Benjamin wept upon Joseph's neck. Joseph kissed all his brothers and wept upon their necks. After that his brothers talked with him (Genesis 45:1–15).

> (Joseph exacted revenge upon his brothers, and along that road of revenge, he had literally put the fear of hell into them. It was Joseph's payback to his brothers for what they had done to him more than twenty years earlier, and for the fear and terror that he had faced as a young teenager and in his first years as an adult. However, Joseph clearly saw the hand of God Almighty in all that had happened, but he was too young and innocent in the ways of men and in the matters of politics to understand that God Almighty was using him to found the Jewish state of Israel, which would follow the judgment of Egypt as a nation, which must come at *the completion of the iniquity—wickedness, immorality and grossly unfair behavior—of the Amorites*.)

When the report, "Joseph's brothers have come," was heard in Pharaoh's house, Pharaoh and his servants were pleased and Pharaoh said to Joseph, "Say to your brothers, 'Do this: load your animals and go back to the land of Canaan. Take your father and your households and come to me, so that I may give you the best of the land of Egypt, and you may enjoy the fat of the land. What is more, take wagons from the land of Egypt for your little ones and for your wives, and bring your father, and come. Do not concern yourselves about your possessions, for the best of all the land of Egypt is yours.'"

So the sons of Israel did as Pharaoh had said. Joseph gave them wagons according to the instruction of Pharaoh, and he gave them provisions for the journey. Each of his brothers were given a set of garments, but to Benjamin he gave five sets of garments and three hundred pieces of silver. To his father Israel he sent: ten donkeys laden with the good things of Egypt, and ten female donkeys laden with grain, bread, and provision for his father on the journey. Then he sent his brothers on their way, and as they were leaving he said to them, "Please do not quarrel along the way."

So they went out of Egypt up to Canaan and came to their father Israel, and they told him, "Joseph is still alive! He is ruler over all Egypt." Israel was stunned; he could not believe them. They told him everything Joseph had said to them, and when he saw the wagons that Joseph had sent to carry him, the spirit of Israel revived. He said, "Enough! My son Joseph is still alive. I must go and see him before I die" (Genesis 45:16–28).

Israel set out on his journey to Egypt with all that he had and came to Beer-sheba. Israel offered sacrifices to God Almighty, the God of his father Isaac. God Almighty spoke to Israel in night visions and said, "Israel, Israel." And he said, "Here I am." Then He said, "I am God Almighty, the God of your father; do not be afraid to go down to Egypt, for *I will make of you a great nation there*. I myself will go down with you to Egypt, and I will also bring you up again; and Joseph will close your eyes with his own hand." Then Israel set out from Beer-sheba; and the sons of Israel carried their father, their little ones, and their wives in the wagons that Pharaoh had sent. They also took their livestock and the goods that they had acquired in Canaan, and they came into Egypt, Israel and all his progeny with him, his sons, and his sons' sons, his daughters, and his sons' daughters; all his offspring he brought with him into Egypt (Genesis 46:1–7).

All the Israelites, Israel and his offspring came to Egypt. Seventy persons of the house of Israel came down to Egypt (Genesis 46:8–27).

Israel (Jacob) goes to Egypt

Israel sent Judah on ahead to Joseph, to lead the way into the land of Goshen. When they came to Goshen, Joseph had his chariot made ready and went up to meet his father Israel in Goshen. He presented himself to him, fell on his neck, and wept there a good while. Israel said to Joseph, "I can die now, having seen for myself that you are still alive." Joseph said to his brothers and to Israel's household, "I will go and tell Pharaoh, and will say to him, 'My brothers and my father's household, who were in the land of Canaan, have come to me. The men are shepherds, for they have been keepers of livestock; and they have brought their flocks, and their herds, and all that they have.' When Pharaoh calls you, and says, 'What is your occupation?' you will say, 'Your servants have been keepers of livestock from our youth until now, both we and our forefathers' — say this in order that you may settle in the land of Goshen, because all shepherds are repugnant to the Egyptians" (Genesis 46:28–34).

Then Joseph went and told Pharaoh, "My father and my brothers, with their flocks and herds and all that they possess, have come from Canaan; they are now in the land of Goshen." Joseph took five from among his brothers and presented them to Pharaoh, who said to Joseph's brothers, "What is your occupation?" And they said, "We are shepherds, as our ancestors were, and we have come to sojourn in the land; for there is no pasture for our flocks because the famine is severe in Canaan. Now, we ask of you to let us settle in the land of Goshen." Then Pharaoh said to Joseph, "Your father and your brothers have come to you. The land of Egypt is before you; settle your father and your brothers in the best part of the land; let them live in the land of Goshen; and if you know that there are capable men among them, put them in charge of my livestock."

Then Joseph brought in his father Israel, and presented him before Pharaoh, and Israel blessed the king of Egypt. Pharaoh asked Israel, "How old are you?" Israel said to Pharaoh, "The years of my sojourn on earth are one hundred and thirty; few and difficult have been the years of my life. They do not compare with the years of the life of my ancestors during their long sojourns." Then Israel blessed Pharaoh again, and went out from his presence. Joseph settled his father and his brothers, and gave them a holding in the land of Egypt, in the best part of the land, in the land of Rameses, as Pharaoh had instructed. And Joseph provided his father, his brothers, and all his father's household with food, according to the number of their dependents (Genesis 47:1–12).

Now there was no food in all the land of Canaan, for the famine was very severe. The land of Egypt and the land of Canaan languished because of the famine. Joseph collected all the money to be found in the land of Egypt and in the land of Canaan, in exchange for the grain that they bought; and Joseph brought the money into Pharaoh's house. When all the money from Egypt and Canaan was spent, the Egyptians came to Joseph, saying, "Give us food! Why should we die before your eyes? Our money is gone." Joseph answered, "If your money is gone, then give me your livestock and I will give you food in exchange for your livestock,"

So they brought their livestock to Joseph and he gave them food in exchange for the horses, the flocks, the herds, and the donkeys. That year Joseph supplied them with food in exchange for their livestock. They came to him the following year, and said to him, "We cannot hide the fact that our money is now spent and the herds of cattle are now Pharaoh's. We have nothing left apart from our bodies and our lands. Must we die before your eyes, both we and our little ones? Buy us and our lands in exchange for food; we and our lands will become slaves to Pharaoh. Just give us seed, so that we may live and not die, and that the lands do not become desolate."

So Joseph bought all the land of Egypt for Pharaoh. All the Egyptians sold their fields, because the famine was severe and the land had became Pharaoh's. As for the people, Joseph made bondslaves of them all throughout the length and breadth of Egypt. Only the land of the priests he did not buy; for the priests had a fixed allowance from Pharaoh and lived on that allowance, therefore they did not sell their lands.

Then Joseph said to the people, "Now that I have bought you and your land for Pharaoh, here is seed for you; sow the land. At the harvests you will give one-fifth to Pharaoh, and four-fifths will be your own, as seed for the field and as food for yourselves, your households, and for your little ones." They said, "You have saved our lives; may it please my lord, we will be slaves to Pharaoh." So Joseph made it a statute concerning the land of Egypt, and it stands to this day, that Pharaoh should receive one fifth of all the produce of Egypt.

So Israel and his progeny settled down in Egypt, in the region of Goshen — also known as the land of Rameses — and they gained possessions in it and were fruitful and multiplied exceedingly. Israel lived in the land of Egypt seventeen years; so the days of Israel, the years of his life, were one hundred forty-seven years (Genesis 47:13–27).

When the time came for Israel's death drew near, he called Joseph to him and said, "If I have found favor with you, put your hand under my thigh and promise to deal loyally and truly with me. Do not bury me in Egypt. When I lie down with my ancestors, carry me out of Egypt and bury me in their burial place." Joseph answered, "I will do as you have requested." And Israel said, "Swear to me"; and Joseph swore to him. Then Israel bowed himself on his bed (Genesis 47:29–31).

After this Joseph was told, "Your father is ill." So he went to him and took his two sons, Manasseh and Ephraim. When Israel was told, "Joseph has come to you," he gathered his strength and sat up in bed. Israel said to Joseph, "God Almighty appeared to me at Luz in the land of Canaan, and He blessed me, and said to me, 'I am going to make you fruitful and increase your numbers; I will make of you a company of peoples, and will give this land to your offspring after you for a perpetual inheritance.' Therefore your sons, who were born to you in the land of Egypt before I came, are now mine; Ephraim and Manasseh will be mine, just as Reuben and Simeon are. As for children born to you after them, they shall be yours. They shall be recorded under the names of their brothers with regard to their inheritance. For when I came from Paddan Aram, Rachel, alas, died in the land of Canaan on the way, while there was still some distance to go and I buried her there on the way to Ephrath" (that is, Bethlehem) Genesis 48:1–7).

When Israel saw Joseph's sons, he said, "Who are these?" Joseph said to his father, "They are my sons, whom God Almighty has given me here." And he said, "Bring them to me that I may bless them." Israel's eyes were dim with age and he could not see well. So Joseph brought them near to Israel; and he kissed them and embraced them. Israel said to Joseph, "I did not expect to see your face; and here God has let me see your children also." Then Joseph removed them from his father's knees, and bowed himself with his face to the ground. Joseph took them both, Ephraim in his right hand toward Israel's left, and Manasseh in his left hand toward Israel's right, and brought them near him. However, Israel stretched out his right hand and laid it on the head of Ephraim, who was the younger, and his left hand on the head of Manasseh, crossing his hands, for Manasseh was the firstborn. He blessed Joseph, and said:—

The God before whom my ancestors Abraham and Isaac walked, the God who has been my shepherd all my life to this day, the angel who has redeemed me from all harm, bless the boys; and in them let my name be perpetuated, and the name of my ancestors Abraham and Isaac; and let them grow into a multitude on the earth (Genesis 48:15–16).

When Joseph saw that his father had his right hand on the head of Ephraim, he was displeased and took his father's hand, to remove it from Ephraim's head to Manasseh's. Joseph said to his father, "Not so, my father! This one is the firstborn so put your right hand on his head." But his father refused, and said, "I know, my son, I know; he also will become a people, and he also will be great. Nevertheless his younger brother will be greater than he, and his offspring will become a multitude of nations." So he blessed them that day, saying, By you Israel will invoke this blessing, saying:—

"God Almighty make you like Ephraim and like Manasseh."

So Israel put Ephraim ahead of Manasseh. Then he said to Joseph, "I am about to die, but God will be with you and will bring you to the land of your ancestors again. I now give to you one portion more than to your brothers, the portion that I took from the hand of the Amorites with my sword and with my bow" (Genesis 48:8–23).

Then Israel called his sons, and said: —

Assemble and hear, O sons of Israel; listen to Israel your father: Reuben, Simeon, Levi, Judah, Dan, Naphtali, Gad, Asher, Issachar, Zebulun, Joseph, and Benjamin. All these are the twelve tribes of Israel, and Israel their father blessed them, blessing each one of them individually with an appropriate blessing (Genesis 49:1).

Then Israel charged them, saying to them, "I am about to be gathered to my people. Bury me with my ancestors—in the cave in the field of Ephron the Hittite, in the cave in the field at Machpelah, near Mamre, in the land of Canaan, in the field that Abraham bought from Ephron the Hittite as a burial site. There Abraham and his wife Sarah were buried; there Isaac and his wife Rebekah were buried; and there I buried Leah—the field and the cave that is in it were purchased from the Hittites." When Jacob ended his charge to his sons, he drew his feet into the bed, breathed his last and was gathered to his people.

Then Joseph threw himself on his father, hugged his face, kissed him and wept over him. Joseph commanded the physicians in his service to embalm his father. So the physicians embalmed Israel; they spent forty days doing this, for that is the time required for embalming. The Egyptians wept for Israel seventy days (Genesis 49:29–50:3).

When the days of mourning for Israel were past, Joseph spoke to the household of Pharaoh, "If now I have found favor with you, please speak to Pharaoh as follows: My father made me swear an oath; he said, 'I am about to die. You will bury me in the tomb that I hewed out for myself in the land of Canaan.' Now, therefore, let me go up to Canaan so that I may bury my father, after which I will return." Pharaoh answered, "Go up, and bury your father, as he made you swear to him" (Genesis 50:4–6).

So Joseph traveled up to Canaan to bury his father. With him went all the servants of Pharaoh, the elders of his household, and all the elders of the land of Egypt, as well as all the household of Joseph, his brothers, and his father's household. Only their children, their flocks, and their herds were left in the land of Goshen. Chariots and charioteers went up with him, it was a very great company. When they came to the threshing floor of Atad, which is beyond the Jordan, they held a very great and sorrowful lamentation; and Joseph observed seven days of heartbreaking mourning for his father. When the inhabitants of Canaan saw the grieving and lamenting, they said, "This is a grievous mourning on the part of the Egyptians." Therefore the place was named Abel-mizraim (Mourning of the Egyptians); it is beyond the Jordan. So Israel's sons did for him as he had instructed. They carried him to the land of Canaan and buried him in the sepulcher of the field at Machpelah, which Abraham had bought as a burial site. After he had buried his father, Joseph returned to Egypt with his brothers and all who had gone up with him for the burial.

Understanding that their father was now dead, Joseph's brothers said, "What if Joseph still bears a grudge against us and pays us back for all the wrong that we did to him?" So the brothers approached Joseph, saying, "Your father gave this instruction before he died, 'Say to Joseph: I beg you, forgive the crime of your brothers and the wrong they did in harming you.'" Joseph shed tears when they spoke to him, then his brothers also wept, fell down before him, and said, "We are here as your slaves." But Joseph said to them, "Do not be afraid! Am I in the place of God? Even though you intended to do harm to me, God intended it for good, in order to preserve many people, as he is doing today. So do not fear; I will provide for you and your little ones." In this way he reassured them, speaking kindly to them (Genesis 50:15–21).

So Joseph remained in Egypt, he and his father's household; and Joseph lived one hundred and ten years. Joseph saw Ephraim's children of the third generation; the children of Machir son of Manasseh were also born on Joseph's knees.

Then Joseph said to his brothers, "I am about to die; but God Almighty will surely come to you, and bring you up out of this land to the land that he swore to Abraham, to Isaac, and to Jacob." So Joseph made the Israelites swear, saying, "When God Almighty comes to you, you will carry up my bones from here." Joseph died, being one hundred and ten years old; he was embalmed and placed in a coffin in Egypt (Genesis 50:15–23).

Egyptian genocide

The names of the sons of Israel who came to Egypt with their father, each one with his household were: Reuben, Simeon, Levi, Judah, Issachar, Zebulun, Benjamin, Dan, Naphtali, Gad and Asher. The number of people born to Israel was seventy. Joseph was already in Egypt. Then Joseph and all his brothers died, along with that whole generation. However, the Israelites were fruitful and prolific; they multiplied and grew exceedingly robust; the land of Egypt was filled with them.

With time, a new king arose over Egypt who had never known Joseph. He said to his people, "Look, the Israelites are more numerous and more powerful than us. Let us deal astutely with them, or they will keep increasing and, in the event of war, join with our enemies and fight against us and escape from the land and we will lose our labor force." Therefore they set taskmasters over them to oppress them with forced labor. However, the more they were oppressed, the more they multiplied and spread, so that the Egyptians came to dread the Israelites. The Egyptians became ruthless in imposing tasks on the Israelites, and made their lives bitter with hard service in mortar and brick and in every kind of field labor. They were ruthless in all the tasks that they imposed on them.

The king of Egypt said to Shiphrah and Puah, the Hebrew midwives, "When you act as midwives to the Hebrew women, and assist them in childbirth, observe at the time of delivery whether it is a boy or a girl. If it is a boy, kill him; if it is a girl, let her live." However, the midwives feared God Almighty and they did not do as Pharaoh commanded and they let the boys live. So the king of Egypt summoned the midwives and said to them:—

Why have you done this, and allowed the boys to live? The midwives said to Pharaoh, "Because the Hebrew women are not like the Egyptian women; they are vigorous and give birth before the midwife comes to them." So God Almighty dealt well with the midwives; and the people multiplied and became very strong. And because the midwives feared God Almighty, He gave them families. Then Pharaoh commanded all his people, "Every boy that is born to the Israelites you will throw into the Nile, but you shall let every girl live" (Exodus 1:1–22).

Now an Israelite man from the house of Levi went and married a Levite woman. The woman conceived and bore a son; and when she saw that he was a fine baby, she hid him for three months. When she could no longer hide him she got a papyrus basket and plastered it with bitumen and pitch; she then put the small child in it and placed it among the reeds on the bank of the river. Miriam, the mother's daughter, stood some distance away and waited to see what would happen to the little child: —

The daughter of Pharaoh came down to bathe at the river, while her attendants walked beside the river. She saw the basket among the reeds and sent her maid to bring it. When she opened it, she saw the child. He was crying, and she took pity on him, "This must be one of the Israelites' children," she said. Then his sister Miriam said to Pharaoh's daughter, "Will I go and get you a nurse from the Israelite women to nurse the child for you?" Pharaoh's daughter said to her, "Yes." So the girl went and called the baby's mother. Pharaoh's daughter said to her, "Take this child and

> *nurse it for me, and I will give you your wages." So the woman took the child and nursed it. When the child grew up, she brought him to Pharaoh's daughter, and she took him as her son. She named him Moses, "Because I drew him out of the water"*
>
> (Exodus 2:1–10).

After Moses had grown up, he one day went out to his people and saw their forced labor and he saw an Egyptian beating a Hebrew, one of his Israelite kinsfolk. Moses looked every which way and seeing no one he killed the Egyptian and buried him in the sand. The next day when he went out he saw two Israelites fighting; and he said to the one who was in the wrong, "Why do you attack your fellow Israelite?" He answered, "Who made you a ruler and judge over us? Do you mean to kill me as you killed the Egyptian yesterday?" Then Moses was afraid and thought, "Surely the thing is known." When Pharaoh heard about it, he sought to kill Moses.

However, Moses fled from Pharaoh and settled in the land of Midian. The priest of Midian had seven daughters and they came to draw water from a well where Moses was sitting. They filled the troughs to water their father's flock, but some shepherds came and drove them away. Moses came to the girls' defense and watered their flock. When they returned home and to their father Reuel (aka Jethro), he said, "How is it that you have come back so quickly today?" They said to their father:—

> *An Egyptian helped us against the shepherds; he even drew water for us and watered the flock." He said to his daughters, "Where is he? Why did you leave the man? Invite him to break bread and eat with us." Moses agreed to stay with the man, and he gave*

Moses his daughter Zipporah in marriage. She bore a son, and he named him Gershom (stranger there); *for he said, "I have been an alien residing in a foreign land."* (Exodus 2:11–22).

In due time, Pharaoh, the king of Egypt died. The Israelites groaned under their slavery burden and cried out in anguish. From their slavery the cry for help rose up to God Almighty and He heard and understood their deep despair. God Almighty remembered His covenant with Abraham, Isaac, and Jacob. The LORD God looked upon the children of Israel and took notice of them (Exodus 2:23–25).

> (The Egyptian slavers were more numerous than the enslaved children of Israel although Pharaoh believed there were more Israelites than Egyptians (Exodus 1:9, 5:5) however, this was only Pharaoh's conjecture. According to historians—who have no real firm scientific data for ancient population numbers—it is estimated there were between four and seven million Egyptians at the time of the Exodus, whereas from the biblical account we can positively arrive at the number of Israelites as being a little less than two million persons. Also, the Egyptian masters had both governing and military power, whereas the enslaved Hebrews virtually only had each other and the clothes they were wearing. However, God Almighty had made promises to the Israelites and had taken notice of their situation in Egypt. And just one man with God Almighty on his side constitutes a

majority. Single handedly, along with ten engineerd catastrophes, God Almighty crushed Egypt, and losing its huge foreign workforce in a single day crashed Egypt's economy. Due to Egypt's treatment of the the children of Israel, the sin of the Amorites—insofar as Egypt is concerned—reached its full measure, which brought the promised reckoning upon Egypt, because whoever *"touches you touches the pupil of His eye"* (Zechariah 2:8).

The catastrophes that befell Egypt are commonly referred to as "plagues," and some of them could well have been "natural" disasters manipulated by the hand of God Almighty to strike at a given time. "Natural" disasters occur at different times and in different countries around the world every year, and many of these are simply judgements in which God Almighty shows His displeasure with the behavior of the inhabitants, similar to the ten disasters that took place in Egypt in rapid succession. The pestilence could have been bubonic plague or similar. A Novel Corona Virus (Covid-19) struck our world in 2019, which infected hundreds of millions of people and has taken the lives of over five million people at this time of writing.

Everyone should be aware that God Almighty rules this world and we should be ever mindful that:—

when God's judgments are in the earth, the inhabitants of the world learn righteousness (Isaiah 26:9.

Righteousness exalts a nation, but sin is a reproach to any people
(Proverbs 14:34).)

Moses: A Man of God

Moses was keeping the flock of his father-in-law Jethro (aka Reuel), the priest of Midian; he led the flock beyond the wilderness and came to Mount Sinai, which is the Mountain of God Almighty. There the angel of the Lord appeared to him in a flame of fire out of a bush; Moses looked, the bush was blazing, but it was not being consumed. Then Moses said to himself, "I must turn aside and look at this astounding sight, and see why the bush is not being burned up." When God Almighty saw that Moses had turned aside to look, He called to him out of the bush, "Moses, Moses!" And Moses responded by saying, "Here I am." Then God Almighty said, "Do not come any closer! Remove the sandals from your feet, for the ground on which you stand is holy ground." God Almighty further said, "I am the God of your father, the God of Abraham, the God of Isaac, and the God of Jacob." Then Moses hid his face, because he was afraid to look at God Almighty (Exodus 3:1-6).

Then God Almighty said, "I have seen the misery of My people who are in Egypt; I have heard the cries because of their taskmasters. I know their sufferings, and I have come down to deliver them from the Egyptians and to bring them out of that land into a good and spacious land, a land flowing with milk and honey, to the country of the Canaanites, the Hittites, the Amorites, the Perizzites, the Hivites, and the Jebusites. The cry of the children of Israel has come to me and I have also seen how the Egyptians oppress them. So come, I will send you to Pharaoh to bring My people out of Egypt." So Moses said to God Almighty, "Who am I that I should go to Pharaoh, and bring the Israelites out of Egypt?" Then God Almighty said, "I will be with you; and this will be the sign for you that it is I who sent you: when you have brought the people out of Egypt, you will worship Me on this mountain."

However, Moses said to God Almighty, "If I come to the Israelites and say to them, 'The LORD God of your ancestors has sent me to you,' and they ask me, 'What is his name?' what will I say to them?" God Almighty said to Moses, "*I am who I am*" (אהיה אשר אהיה). He further said, "This is what you will say to the children of Israel, '*I am* —(אהיה)— has sent me to you.'" God Almighty also said to Moses, "This is what you will say to the Israelites, 'The LORD, the God of your ancestors, the God of Abraham, the God of Isaac, and the God of Jacob, has sent me to you': *"This is my name forever, and this my title for all generations"* (Exodus 3:15).

> (In Hebrew, the name *"I am who I am"* — (אהיה אשר אהיה) — means: "I am who I am; I will become whomever I want to become and will become whatever I want to become; I will do whatever I want whenever I want." Almighty God then gave a shortened version of His name — *"I am"* (אהיה) — which means all of the above. It is therefore a rather pointless exercise for Man trying to tell God what He can or cannot do.)

God Almighty continued and said to Moses: "Go and assemble the elders of Israel, and say to them, 'The LORD, the almighty God of your ancestors, the God of Abraham, of Isaac, and of Jacob, has appeared to me, saying: I have taken notice of you and seen what has been done to you in Egypt. I declare to you that I will bring you up out of the misery of Egypt, to the land of the Canaanites, the Hittites, the Amorites, the Perizzites, the Hivites, and the Jebusites, a land flowing with milk and honey.' They will listen to your voice; and you and the elders of Israel will go to the king of Egypt and say to him, 'The LORD, the God of the Hebrews, has met with us; let us now go a three days' journey into the wilderness, so that we may sacrifice to the LORD our God.' I know, however, that the king of Egypt will not let you go unless compelled to do so by a strong hand. So I will stretch out My hand and strike Egypt with some wonders that I will perform. After that he will let you go and I will bring My people into such favor with the Egyptians that, when you go, you will not go empty-handed. Every woman will ask her neighbor and any woman living in the neighbor's house for jewelry of silver and of gold, and clothing, and you will put them on your sons and on your daughters; and so you will plunder the Egyptians."

Then Moses answered, "But suppose they do not believe me or listen to me, but say, 'God Almighty did not appear to you.'" The LORD then said to him, "What is that in your hand?" Moses said, "A staff." And God Almighty said, "Throw it on the ground." So Moses threw the staff on the ground, and it became a snake; and Moses drew back from it. Then God Almighty said to Moses, "Reach out your hand, and seize it by the tail"—so he reached out his hand and grasped it by the tail, and it became a staff in his hand— "so that they may believe that the LORD, the almighty God of their ancestors, the God of Abraham, the God of Isaac, and the God of Jacob, has appeared to you."

Furthermore, God Almighty said to Moses, "Put your hand inside your cloak." Moses put his hand into his cloak;

and when he took it out, his hand was leprous, as white as snow. Then God Almighty said, "Put your hand back into your cloak." So Moses put his hand back into his cloak, and when he took it out, it was restored like the rest of his body. God Almighty said, "If they will not believe you or take notice of the first sign, they may believe the second sign. If they will not believe even these two signs or heed you, take some water from the Nile and pour it on the dry ground and the water that you take from the River will become blood on the dry ground."

However, Moses said to God Almighty, "O my Lord, I have never been eloquent, not in the past or even now that you have spoken to me; I am slow of speech and tongue." Then God Almighty said to Moses, "Who gives speech to mortals? Who makes them mute or deaf, seeing or blind? Is it not I, the Lord God? Now go, and I will be with your mouth and teach you all that you are to speak." Nevertheless, Moses said, "O my Lord, please send someone else." Then the anger of God Almighty was kindled against him and He said, "What of your brother Aaron, the Levite? I know that he can speak fluently; even now he is coming out to meet you, and when he sees you his heart will be glad. You will speak to him and put the words in his mouth; and I will be with your mouth and with his mouth, and I will teach you what you will do. He will certainly speak for you to the people; he will serve as a mouth for you, and you will serve as God for him. Take in your hand this staff, with which you will perform the wonders" (Exodus 4:1–17).

> (Moses was in Midian and Aaron was in Egypt, yet God Almighty *saw* Aaron coming to meet Moses in the wilderness.

We should understand that God Almighty not only knows the future, but He actually sees the future as happening now, and this should inspire us to lean more upon God Almighty in every circumstance.)

Moses went back to his father-in-law Jethro and said to him, "Please let me go back to my people in Egypt and see whether they are still living." And Jethro said to Moses, "Go in peace." Then God Almighty said to Moses in Midian, "Go back to Egypt; for all those who were seeking your life are dead." So Moses took Zipporah his wife and his two sons, put them on a donkey and journeyed back to Egypt; and Moses carried the staff of God Almighty in his hand.

And God Almighty said to Moses, "When you go back to Egypt, see that you show Pharaoh all the wonders that I have put in your power; but I will harden Pharaoh's heart, so that he will not let the people go. Then you will say to Pharaoh, 'Thus says the LORD:—

Israel is My firstborn son, and I say to you, "Let My son go that he may serve Me." If you refuse to let him go, indeed, I will kill your firstborn son

(Exodus 4:23).

On the way, at a place where they spent the night, God Almighty met Moses and tried to kill him because he had not circumcised his youngest son. So Zipporah took a flint knife and cut off her son's foreskin, and touched Moses' feet with it, and said, "Truly you are a bridegroom of blood to me!" So God Almighty let him alone. It was then that Zipporah said, *"A bridegroom of blood by circumcision"* (Exodus 4:25–26).

God Almighty said to Aaron, "Go into the wilderness to meet Moses." So Aaron went; and he met Moses at the Mountain of God and kissed him. Moses told Aaron all the words of God Almighty with which He had sent him, and all the signs with which He had been charged. Then they both went and assembled all the elders of the Israelites. Aaron spoke all the words that God Almighty had spoken to Moses, and he performed the signs in the sight of the people. The people believed him, and when they heard that God Almighty had listened to the pain of the children of Israel and that he had seen their misery, they bowed down and worshiped.

After that Moses and Aaron went to Pharaoh and said, "This is what the LORD, the Most High God of Israel says to you, 'Let My people go, so that they may celebrate a festival to me in the wilderness.'" However, Pharaoh said, "Who is the LORD, that I should listen to him and let Israel go? I do not know the LORD, and I will not let Israel go." Then they said, "God Almighty, the LORD God of the Hebrews has revealed Himself to us; let us go a three days' journey into the wilderness to sacrifice to Him, or He will fall upon us with plague or sword." However, Pharaoh said to Moses and Aaron, "Why are you taking the people away from their work? Get to your labors!" The king of Egypt continued, "The Israelites are more in number than the people of the land, and you want them to stop working!"

That day Pharaoh instructed the taskmasters of the Israelites, as well as their Israelite supervisors, "No longer give the people straw to make bricks, let them go and get straw for themselves. However, you will demand from them the same quantity of bricks as they have made previously; do not diminish the quantity, for they are lazy; that is why they cry, 'Let us go and offer a sacrifice to our God.' Let their work load be heavier; then they will work without paying attention to deceptive words."

So the taskmasters and the Israelite supervisors went out and said to the Israelites, "Thus says Pharaoh, 'I will not give you straw. Go get straw for yourselves, but your work load will not be lessened at all.'" So the Israelites scattered throughout the land, to find stubble for straw. The taskmasters were insistent, saying, "Complete your work, the same quota as when you were given straw." The Israelite supervisors of the people, whom the taskmasters had put over the slaves, were beaten, and then asked, "Why did you not produce the required number of bricks yesterday and today, as you did previously?"

Then the supervisors came to Pharaoh and said, "Why do you treat your servants like this? No straw is given to us, yet they say, 'Make bricks!' Look how we are beaten! You are being unfair to your own people." Pharaoh said, "You are lazy, lazy; that is why you say, 'Let us go and sacrifice to the LORD God.' Get back to work. No straw will be given to you, but you will still produce the same quota of bricks." The supervisors understood that they were in dire trouble when told, "You will not reduce your daily quota of bricks." After they left Pharaoh, they came upon Moses and Aaron who were waiting to meet them. The supervisors said to them, "The LORD look upon you and judge! You have brought us into a bad light with Pharaoh and his officials, and have given them a weapon to kill us" (Exodus 4:18–5:21).

Moses turned to the LORD and said, "O LORD, why have you mistreated this people? Why did you ever send me? Since I first came to Pharaoh to speak in your name, he has mistreated this people and You have done nothing to deliver your people." Then the LORD said to Moses, "Now you will see what I will do. Indeed, by My mighty hand Pharaoh will let them go; by My mighty hand he will drive them out of Egypt" (Exodus 5:22–6:1).

The LORD God then spoke to Moses and said: "I am the LORD. I appeared to Abraham, Isaac, and Jacob as God Almighty (אל שדי), but by my name 'Yahweh' (יהוה – most English translations *"The LORD"*) I did not make myself known to them. I also established my covenant with them, to give them the land of Canaan, the land in which they lived as aliens. I have also heard the groaning of the children of Israel whom the Egyptians are holding as slaves, and I have remembered my covenant. So, say to the Israelites, 'I am the LORD, I will free you from the burdens of the Egyptians and deliver you from being slaves. I will redeem you with an outstretched arm and with mighty acts of power and judgment. I will take you as My people, and I will be your God. You will know that I am the LORD your God, who has freed you from the burdens of the Egyptians. I will bring you into the land that I swore to give to Abraham, Isaac, and Jacob; I will give it to you for an everlasting possession. I am the LORD.'" Moses told this to the children of Israel; but they would not listen to him, because of their broken spirit and the brutal slavery that they were subjected to.

Then the LORD God Almighty spoke to Moses, "Go and tell Pharaoh king of Egypt to let the Israelites go out of his land." But Moses said to God Almighty, "The Israelites are not listening to me; how then will Pharaoh listen to such a poor speaker?" But God Almighty spoke to Moses and

Aaron and gave them instructions regarding the children of Israel, and Pharaoh the king of Egypt, demanding that he free the children of Israel from the land of Egypt (Exodus 6:2–13).

Now these are the families of the Levites according to their genealogies. Amram married his aunt Jochebed and she gave birth to Aaron and Moses. The length of Amram's life was one hundred and thirty-seven years (Exodus 6:19–20). Aaron married Elisheba, the daughter of Amminadab and sister of Nahshon, and she gave birth to Nadab, Abihu, Eleazar, and Ithamar (Exodus 6:23). Aaron's son Eleazar married one of the daughters of Putiel, and she gave birth to Phinehas, who, because of his zeal for God Almighty he had a covenant of peace bestowed upon him by the Lord. So these then are the heads of the ancestral houses of the Levites by their families.

It was to this same Aaron and Moses that God Almighty said, "Bring the Israelites out of the land of Egypt, company by company." It was this same Moses and Aaron who spoke to Pharaoh to bring the children of Israel out of Egypt. On the day that God Almighty spoke to Moses in the land of Egypt, He said to him, "I am the Lord; tell Pharaoh all that I am telling you." But Moses said to the Lord, "Because I am such a poor speaker, why should Pharaoh listen to me?"

Then the Lord said to Moses, "Look, I have made you like God Almighty to Pharaoh, and your brother Aaron will be your prophet. You will declare all that I command you, and your brother Aaron will tell Pharaoh to let the children of Israel go out of his land. However, I will harden Pharaoh's heart, and I will multiply my signs and wonders in Egypt. When Pharaoh does not listen to you, I will lay my hand heavily upon the land of Egypt and bring My people, the children of Israel, company by company, out of Egypt by great acts of power and judgment. The Egyptians will know that I am the LORD God Almighty when I stretch out my hand against their land and bring the children of Israel out from their midst." Moses and Aaron did exactly as God Almighty instructed them. Moses was eighty years old and Aaron eighty-three when they spoke to Pharaoh (Exodus 6:24–7:7).

Moses and Aaron spoke with Pharaoh, and Moses, as a sign of his authority, threw down his staff and it turned into a serpent (snake). Pharaoh's magicians and wise men copied the act and threw down their rods, which all turned into serpents, but the staff of Moses swallowed them all up. Pharaoh refused to let the Israelite slaves go and God Almighty got more serious with His signs while at the same time strengthening Pharaoh's determination not to let the Israelites go.

Moses and Aaron before Pharaoh

The first sign with which God Almighty showed his awesome power in Egypt was one of BLOOD. The River Nile was Egypt's preeminent deity (god) and the heads of Pharaoh's household would go to the River each morning, early, to bathe and recite prayers. At God Almighty's command, Moses struck the water of the Nile with his staff in the presence of Pharaoh's officials, and the water turned into BLOOD and all the fish in the River died. There was only stinking, undrinkable water throughout the land; even the water in the vessels of wood and in the vessels of stone was BLOOD, but the Egyptian magicians did the same by their magic arts, so Pharaoh's heart remained hard—just as the LORD had predicted. Pharaoh was unperturbed and went home. A week passed and people were still digging for water to drink after God Almighty turned the River into BLOOD (Exodus 7:25).

God Almighty then said to Moses, Go to Pharaoh and say, "This is what the LORD says: Let My people go so that they may serve Me, and if you refuse to let them go, I will smite your land with FROGS and the Nile will swarm with FROGS. They will come into your house and into your bedroom and onto your bed, and into your servants' houses and those of your people. They will come up into the ovens and into the kneading bowls."

At that time the LORD said to Moses, "Say to Aaron, 'Stretch out your hand with your staff over the rivers, the canals, and the pools, and make FROGS come up on the land of Egypt.'" So Aaron stretched out his hand and his staff over the waters of Egypt; and FROGS came up and covered the land. However, the magicians also did the same by their magic arts and they brought frogs up on the land of Egypt.

Then Pharaoh called Moses and Aaron and said, "Negotiate with the LORD to take away the **FROGS** from me and my people. I will let the Israelites go and sacrifice to the LORD." Moses said to Pharaoh, "Please tell me when I am to intervene for you, for your servants and for your people, that the **FROGS** might be cut off from you and your people and be left only in the Nile." And Pharaoh said, "Tomorrow." Moses then said, "It will be as you say, so you may know that there is none like the LORD our God. The **FROGS** will go from you and your houses and from your servants and your people. They will only be left in the Nile."

So Moses and Aaron went out from Pharaoh, and Moses cried to the LORD about the **FROGS** just like he had agreed with Pharaoh; and the LORD did according to the word of Moses. The **FROGS** died out in the houses, the courtyards, and the fields. The Egyptians gathered them together in heaps, and the land stank. However, when Pharaoh saw there was a respite from the **FROGS**, he hardened his heart and would not listen further, exactly as the LORD had said (Exodus 8:13–15).

Now the LORD said to Moses, "Say to Aaron, 'Stretch out your rod, and strike the dust of the land, so that it may become **GNATS** (small two-winged biting flies similar to mosquitos) throughout all the land of Egypt'" and they did as the LORD said. Aaron stretched out his hand with his rod and struck the dust of the earth, and it became **GNATS** on man and beast. All the dust of the land became **GNATS** throughout all the land of Egypt.

Now the magicians worked with their magic to bring forth **GNATS**, but they could not. There were **GNATS** on both man and beast. Then the magicians said to Pharaoh, "This is the finger of the LORD God Almighty." The king's heart grew hard and he did not heed them, just as the LORD had said (Exodus 8:18–19).

At that time the LORD said to Moses, "Get up early in the morning and present yourself before Pharaoh, as he goes out to the water, and say to him, 'This is what the LORD says: Let my people go, so that they may worship Me. And if you will not let My people go, I will send swarms of FLIES on you, on your officials, and on your people, and into your houses; and the houses of the Egyptians will be filled with swarms of FLIES; so also the land where they live. However, on that day I will set apart the land of Goshen, where My people live, so that no swarms of FLIES will be there, that you may know that I the LORD am in the midst of this land. I will make a distinction between My people and your people and this sign will appear tomorrow.'" The LORD did so, and great swarms of FLIES came into the house of Pharaoh and into the houses of his officials'; all of the land of Egypt was ruined because of the FLIES (Exodus 8:20–24).

Then Pharaoh sent for Moses and Aaron, and said to them, "Go, sacrifice to your God within the land." But Moses said, "It would not be right to do so; for the sacrifices that we offer to the LORD our God are offensive to the Egyptians. If we offer in the sight of the Egyptians sacrifices that are offensive to them, will they not stone us? We must go a three days' journey into the wilderness and sacrifice to the LORD our God as He commands." So Pharaoh said, "I will let you go to sacrifice to the LORD your God in the wilderness, provided you do not go very far away. Pray for me." Then Moses said, "When I leave you, I will pray to the LORD that the swarms of FLIES may depart tomorrow from Pharaoh, from his officials, and from his people; only do not let Pharaoh deal falsely again by not letting the people go to sacrifice to the LORD God. So Moses went out from Pharaoh and prayed to the LORD and the LORD did as Moses asked: He removed the swarms of **FLIES** from Pharaoh, from his officials, and from his people; not one remained. However, Pharaoh hardened his heart again and would not let the Israelites go (Exodus 8:25–29).

Then the LORD said to Moses, "Go to Pharaoh, and say to him, 'This is what the LORD, the Almighty God of the Hebrews says: Let My people go, so that they may worship Me. But if you refuse and still hold them, the hand of the LORD God will strike your livestock in the field: the horses, the donkeys, the camels, the herds, and the flocks with a deadly **PESTILENCE**. However, the LORD will make a distinction between the livestock of Israel and the livestock of Egypt, so that nothing that belongs to the children of Israel will die.'"

The LORD set a time, saying, "Tomorrow I will do this thing in the land." The next day God Almighty did all that He said; all the livestock of the Egyptians died, but of the livestock of the Israelites not one died. Pharaoh inquired and found that not one of the livestock of the Israelites was dead. However, the heart of Pharaoh was hardened and he would not let the children of Israel go (Exodus 9:1–7).

Then the LORD said to Moses and Aaron, "Take handfuls of soot from the kiln and let Moses throw it in the air in the sight of Pharaoh. It will become fine dust all over the land of Egypt, and it will cause festering **BOILS** on humans and animals throughout the whole land." So Aaron and Moses took soot from the kiln, and stood before Pharaoh, and Moses threw it in the air, and it caused festering BOILS on humans and animals. The magicians could not stand before Moses because of the BOILS, for the BOILS afflicted the magicians as well as all the other Egyptians. However, the LORD hardened the heart of Pharaoh, and he would not listen, just as the LORD had said (Exodus 9:8–12).

Then the LORD God said to Moses, "Rise early in the morning and present yourself before Pharaoh and say to him, 'This is what the LORD, the Almighty God of the Hebrews says: Let My people go, so that they may worship Me, for this time I will send my plagues upon you yourself, upon your officials, and upon all your people, so that you may know that there is no one like Me in all the earth. I could already have struck you and your people with pestilence, and you would have been cut off from the earth. However, this is the reason why I have let you live: to show you My power and to make My name reverberate throughout all the earth. You exalt yourself against My people and will not let them go. So at this time tomorrow I will cause the heaviest HAIL to fall that has ever fallen in Egypt from the day it was founded until now. Have your livestock and everything in the field brought to a safe place; every human or animal that is in the field that is not brought under shelter will die when the HAIL comes down.'" Pharaoh's officials who feared the word of the LORD hurried their slaves and livestock off to a safe place. Those who did not regard the word of the LORD left their slaves and livestock in the fields.

Then God Almighty said to Moses, "Stretch out your hand toward heaven so that HAIL may fall on the whole land of Egypt, on humans and animals and all the plants of the fields in the land." Then Moses stretched out his staff toward heaven, and the LORD sent thunder and HAIL, and fire came down on the earth. The LORD rained HAIL on the land of Egypt; there was HAIL with fire flashing continually in the midst of it, such heavy HAIL as had never fallen in all the land of Egypt since its founding. The HAIL struck down everything that was in the open fields throughout the land, both human and animal. The HAIL also struck down all the plants of the fields, and shattered every tree in the fields. Only in the land of Goshen, where the children of Israel were, was there no HAIL (Exodus 9:13–26).

Then Pharaoh summoned Moses and Aaron, and said to them, "I have sinned; the LORD is in the right and I and my people are in the wrong. Pray to the LORD! Enough of the LORD's thunder and hail! I will let you go; you need stay no longer." Moses said to him, "As soon as I have left the city I will stretch out my hands to the LORD God; the thunder will cease and there will be no more HAIL, so that you may know that the earth is the LORD's. However, as for you and your officials, I know that you do not yet fear the LORD our God." (Now the flax and the barley were ruined, because the barley was in the ear and the flax was in bud, but the wheat and the spelt were not ruined, because they are late crops.) So Moses went out from Pharaoh; he left the city and stretched out his hands to the LORD, then the thunder and the HAIL ceased and the rain no longer came down on the land. When Pharaoh saw that the rain, the HAIL, and the thunder had ceased, he sinned again and hardened his heart, both he and his officials. The heart of Pharaoh was hardened and he would not let the children of Israel go, just as the LORD had spoken through Moses (Exodus 9:27–35).

Moses and Aaron before Pharaoh

At that time God Almighty said to Moses, "Go to Pharaoh; for I have hardened his heart and the heart of his officials, in order that I may show these signs of mine among them, and that you may tell your children and grandchildren how I ridiculed the Egyptians and what signs I have done among them; so that you may know I am the LORD."

So Moses and Aaron went to Pharaoh, and said, "This is what the LORD, the God Almighty of the Hebrews says, 'How long will you refuse to humble yourself before Me? Let My people go, so that they may worship Me. For if you refuse to let My people go, tomorrow I will bring LOCUSTS onto your land. They will cover the surface of your country, so that no one will be able to see the land. They will devour the last remnant left to you after the HAIL, and they will devour every tree of yours that grows in the field. They will fill your houses, and the houses of all your officials and of all the Egyptians—something that neither your parents nor your grandparents have ever seen, from the day they were born to this day.'" Then they turned and went out from Pharaoh (Exodus 10:1–6).

Pharaoh's officials said to him, "How long will this man be a snare to us? Let the children of Israel go, so that they may worship the LORD their God; do you not yet understand that Egypt is ruined?" So Moses and Aaron were brought back to Pharaoh, and he said to them, "Go, worship the LORD your God! However, which ones are to go?" Moses said, "We will go with our young and our old; with our sons and our daughters and with our flocks and herds, because we have the LORD's festival to celebrate." Pharaoh said to them, "The LORD indeed will need to be with you if ever I let your children go with you! It is obvious that you have an evil purpose in mind. No, never! Your men may go and worship the LORD, for that is what you are asking." And Moses and Aaron were driven out from Pharaoh's presence.

Then the LORD said to Moses, "Stretch out your hand over the land of Egypt so that the LOCUSTS will come upon it and eat every plant in the land, all that the HAIL has left." So Moses stretched out his staff over the land, and the LORD brought an east wind upon the land all that day and all that night. When morning came, the east wind had brought the LOCUSTS, and the LOCUSTS came upon all the land of Egypt and settled on the whole country, such a dense swarm of LOCUSTS as had never been before, nor ever will be again. They covered the surface of the land, so that the land was black and moving; and they ate all the plants and all the fruit of the trees that the HAIL had left; nothing green remained, no tree and no plant in the field remained in all the land of Egypt. Pharaoh hastily summoned Moses and Aaron and said, "I have sinned against the LORD your God, and against you. Please forgive my sin just this once, and pray to the LORD your God that He remove this deadly plague from me." So they went out from Pharaoh and prayed to the LORD and the LORD changed the east wind into a very strong west wind, which lifted the LOCUSTS and drove them into the Red Sea; no LOCUSTS were left in all the land of Egypt. However, the LORD hardened Pharaoh's heart again, and he would not let the Israelites go (Exodus 10:7–20).

So the LORD God said to Moses, "Stretch out your hand toward heaven so that there may be DARKNESS over the land of Egypt, a DARKNESS that can be felt." And so Moses stretched out his hand toward heaven, and there was dense

DARKNESS in all the land of Egypt for three days. People could not see one another, and for three days they could not move from where they were; but all the Israelites had light where they lived. Then Pharaoh sent for Moses, and said, "Go, worship the LORD. Only your flocks and your herds will remain behind. Even your children may go with you." But Moses said, "You must also let us have sacrifices and burnt offerings to sacrifice to the LORD our God. Our livestock also must go with us; we will not leave one hoof behind, for we must choose some of them for the worship of the LORD our God, and we will not know which ones until we get there." However, God Almighty hardened Pharaoh's heart, and he was unwilling to let them go. At that time Pharaoh said to Moses, "Get out from before me! Take care that you do not see my face again, for on the day you see my face you will die." Moses said, "Just as you say! I will not see your face again" (Exodus 10:21–29).

The LORD God Almighty then said to Moses, "I will bring one more plague upon Pharaoh and the land of Egypt; afterwards he will let you go; indeed, not only will he let you go, but he will drive you away. Tell the Israelites that every man is to ask his neighbor and every woman is to ask her neighbor for objects of silver and gold," and the LORD God Almighty gave the people favor in the sight of the Egyptians. Moreover, Moses himself was a man of great importance in the land of Egypt, both in the sight of Pharaoh's officials and in the sight of the people.

Moses then said to Pharaoh, "This is what the LORD God Almighty says: About midnight I will go throughout Egypt. Every FIRSTBORN in the land of Egypt will die, from the FIRSTBORN of Pharaoh who sits on the throne to the FIRSTBORN of the female slave who is behind the hand mill, and all the FIRSTBORN of the livestock. Then there will be a loud cry throughout the whole land of Egypt, such as has never been or will ever be again. However, not even a dog will growl at any of the Israelites—not at the people, nor at their animals—so you may know the LORD of the whole earth makes a distinction between Egypt and Israel. Then all these officials of yours will come to me and bow low saying, 'Leave us, you and all the people who follow you.' After that I will leave." And in hot anger Moses left Pharaoh.

Then God Almighty said to Moses, "Pharaoh will not listen to you, in order that my wonders may be multiplied in the land of Egypt." Moses and Aaron performed all these wonders before Pharaoh; but the LORD hardened Pharaoh's heart, and he did not let the children of Israel leave his land.

Then the LORD God Almighty said to Moses and Aaron: *This month will mark for you the beginning of the months; it will be the first month of the year for you* (Exodus 12:2).

(The first month of the Hebrew year at that time was *Aviv*—now called *Nisan*—which is at variance with the Jewish New Year being celebrated worldwide on the first day of *Tishrei*, which coincides with parts of September and October on the Gregorian calendar. Ultra-Orthodox Rabbis hold sovereign control over religious days and events, and Israel's governments are beholden to them; the approximately eleven percent ultra-Orthodox (haredi) population in Israel has become a state within a state with its own rules of conduct, seeing itself as free from the government and the laws of the land.

Long ago some traditional Jewish dates of remembrance were shuffled around by the Rabbis because observing them on their original days could lead to Yeshua (Jesus) being recognized as the Jewish Messiah. Aeons ago Rabbis and sages forbade the Haftorah reading of Isaiah 53 in synagogues. (Isaiah 53 is a clear portrayal of the suffering Messiah and is today known as the forbidden chapter; and until the coming of of Yeshua (Jesus) Jewish sages and rabbis emphatically agreed that the chapter was a prophecy about the Messiah. Now it is hidden.) Yeshua (Jesus) did not meet the preconceived expectations of the Rabbis, he did not come as a warrior ready to establish Israel as the preeminent kingdom, instead he came as a humble servant to the masses.

Religious leaders also colluded together to move days and dates around in order to place barriers before Jews, hindering them from understanding that Yeshua (Jesus) is the Messiah. And in our last passage we have a divinely decreed first month, in which Yeshua (Jesus), God Almighty's Sacrificial Lamb is crucified on the fourteenth day, but the divine decree for New Year has been buried by the Rabbis, relegated to being the first month of the civil year and the seventh month of *Tishrei* (when counting from Nissan) has, by rabbinical decree, declared to be the start of the religious year, and which removes the linkage to the crucifixion of God Almighty's *only begotten Son*.)

The LORD God said to Moses and Aaron: —

Tell the whole congregation of Israel that on the tenth day of this month they are to take a lamb for each family, a lamb for each household. If a household is too small for a whole lamb, it should join its closest neighbor to obtain one; the lamb will be divided in proportion to the number of people who eat of it. The lamb must be without blemish, a year-old male; you may take it from the sheep flock or from the goat herd. You will keep it until the fourteenth day of this month; then the whole assembled congregation of Israel will kill it at twilight. They will take some of the blood and put it on the two doorposts and the lintel of the houses in which they eat it. They will eat the lamb that same night; they will eat it roasted over the fire with unleavened bread and bitter herbs. Do not eat any of it raw or boiled in water, but only roasted over the fire, with its head, legs, and inner organs. You must let none of it remain until the morning; anything that does remain until the morning you must burn. You will eat it with your loins girded, your sandals on your feet, and your staff in your hand; and you will eat it hurriedly. It is the passover of the LORD. For I will pass through the land of Egypt that night, and I will strike down every FIRSTBORN in the land of Egypt, both humans and animals; and on all the gods of Egypt I will execute judgments: I am the LORD. The blood will be a sign for you on the houses where you live. When I see the blood, I will pass over you and no plague will destroy you when I strike the land of Egypt" (Exodus 12:2–13).

Moses and Aaron continued: "This day will be a day of remembrance for you. You will celebrate it as a festival to God Almighty throughout your generations; you will observe it as a perpetual ordinance. Seven days you will eat unleavened bread; on the first day you will remove all leaven from your houses; whoever eats leavened bread from the first day until the seventh day will be cut off from Israel. On the first day you will hold a holy assembly, and on the seventh day you will also hold a holy assembly; no work can be done on those solemn days; only what everyone must eat, that alone may be prepared. You will observe the festival of unleavened bread, for on this very day I brought all the children of Israel out of the land of Egypt: you will observe this day throughout your generations as a statute forever. In the first month, from the evening of the fourteenth day until the evening of the twenty-first day, you will eat unleavened bread. For seven days no leaven will be found in your houses; whoever eats what is leavened will be cut off from the congregation of Israel, whether an alien or a native Israelite. You will eat nothing leavened; in all your dwelling places you will eat unleavened bread (Exodus 12:14–20).

Moses then called all the elders of Israel and said to them, "Go, select lambs for your families, and slaughter the passover lamb. Take a bunch of hyssop, dip it in the blood that is collected in a basin, and touch the lintel and the two doorposts with the blood. None of you can go outside the door of your house until morning. For the LORD God Almighty will pass through to strike down the Egyptians; when he sees the blood on the lintel and on the two doorposts He will pass over those doors and not allow the destroyer to enter your houses to strike you down. You will observe this rite as a statute forever, you and your children. When you come to the land that the LORD God Almighty has promised to give you, you must keep this observance. When your children ask, 'What do you mean by observing this rite?' you will say, 'It is the passover sacrifice to the LORD, for He passed over the houses of the Israelites in Egypt during the night and struck down the Egyptians but spared our houses.'" And the people bowed down and worshiped. The Israelites then went and did exactly as the LORD God Almighty had commanded Moses and Aaron.

At midnight the LORD struck down all the FIRSTBORN in the land of Egypt, from the FIRSTBORN of Pharaoh who sat on his throne to the FIRSTBORN of the prisoner who was in the dungeon, and all the FIRSTBORN of the livestock. Pharaoh arose in the night, he and all his officials and all the Egyptians; and there was a very loud cry in Egypt, for there was not a house without someone having been struck dead. Then Pharaoh hastily summoned Moses and Aaron in the night and said to them, "Go away from my people, both you and all the children of Israel! Go, worship the LORD. Take your flocks and your herds and be gone; and bring a blessing on me too!"

The Egyptians pressed the children of Israel to make haste in departing from the land, saying, "We will all be dead." So the Israelites took their unleavened dough in their kneading bowls, wrapped up in their cloaks and carried on their shoulders. The Israelites had done as Moses told

Moses and Aaron before Pharaoh

them; they had asked the Egyptians for jewelry of silver and gold, and for clothing and the LORD had given the Israelites favor in the sight of the Egyptians, so that they gave them what they asked for. And so Israel plundered the Egyptians (Exodus 11:1–12:36).

> (About 3,500 years ago (scholars differ on the exact timeline) the Israelites—the descendants of Abraham through his son Isaac left Egypt after more than four hundred years—of which many were spent as slaves of the Egyptians—and journeyed toward Canaan. The Hebrew Bible informs us that in total, but excluding the tribe of Levi:—
>
> *from twenty years old and upward,* ***everyone able to go to war in Israel****—their whole number was six hundred three thousand five hundred fifty. The Levites, however, were not numbered by their ancestral tribe along with them"* (Numbers 1:45–47).

This amount was not the number of Israelites that came out from Egypt, these were only the warriors, men fit for waging war. As to be expected, some scholars dispute the numbers, but the Hebrew Bible definitively states that the number of those able *"to bear arms"* was six hundred three thousand five hundred fifty.

As in most populations, females would make up approximately fifty – fifty-one percent of the population, so we can now safely double the number given for those males able to bear arms, which gives us one million two hundred seven thousand one hundred. However, we are not finished. We must add to that number all the males and females below the twenty-year conscription age, and also of those who were either too old or too feeble to bear arms. There must surely have been about the same number as those who bore arms, therefore we add another six hundred three thousand five hundred fifty, which gives us a rough tally of one million, eight hundred ten thousand, six hundred and fifty, plus twenty-two thousand Levite males from one month old and upwards (Numbers 3:39) and the same number for females of the Levite tribe, giving us an approximate total of one million, eight hundred fifty-four thousand, six hundred and fifty Israelites (1,854,650) coming out of Egypt.

Critics will likely say there is no evidence that such a large number would have come out from Egypt because, unlike modern-day picnickers who despoil every eye-pleasing spot they find, the Israelites did not leave heaps of plastic bags, bottles and soda cans. Cooking pots and other utensils brought from Egypt would have been taken into Canaan, and at the end of their journey God Almighty told the Israelites:—

I have led you forty years in the wilderness. Your clothes have not

worn out on you, and your sandals have not worn out on your feet
(Deuteronomy 29:5).

Cooking utensils, clothing and footwear lasted throughout the journey so, apart from the faithless generation from the age of twenty years and upwards, which subsequently died out over a period of forty years and buried in the vast area of the wilderness, there would have been little evidence of such a horde having passed through.

Of the one million, eight hundred fifty-four thousand, six hundred and fifty (1,854,650) Israelites who came out of Egypt, an entire generation from the age of twenty years upwards was buried in the wilderness during Israel's forty-years of wandering in it—one year for every day the faithless spies spent scouting out the land of Canaan:—

And your children will be shepherds in the wilderness for forty years, and will suffer for your faithlessness, until the last of your dead bodies lies in the wilderness. According to the number of the days in which you spied out the land, forty days, for every day a year, you will bear your iniquity, forty years, and you will know my displeasure." I the Lord *God Almighty have spoken; surely I will do thus to all this wicked congregation that gathered together against me: in this wilderness they will come to a full end, and there they will die* (Numbers 14:33–35).

The LORD's anger was kindled on that day and he swore, saying, "Surely none of the people who came up out of Egypt, **from twenty years old and upward**, *will see the land that I swore to give to Abraham, to Isaac, and to Jacob, because they have not unreservedly followed me— none except Caleb son of Jephunneh the Kenizzite and Joshua son of Nun, for they have unreservedly followed the LORD God Almighty." And the LORD's anger was kindled against Israel, and he made them wander in the wilderness for forty years, until all the generation that had done evil in the sight of the God Almighty had disappeared* (Numbers 32:10–13).

Assuming that over the forty years the Israelites continued to reproduce like the faithless generation that fell in the wilderness, we could reasonably expect to have an approximate Israelite population of somewhere around one million, eight hundred thirty-two thousand, six hundred and fifty (1,832,650) who entered upon the conquest of the Promised Land under the leadership of General Joshua. We will get to all this soon enough.)

Catch us if you can

People still speak of the plagues of Egypt today, more than three thousand-plus years after the advent. God Almighty's *"hand is not shortened, that it cannot save, or His ear dull, that it cannot hear"* (Isaiah 59:1). And what was true then still holds true today.

The disasters that God Almighty brought upon Egypt brought freedom to the Israelites, the sons of Jacob. This great multitude of people left Egypt with their flocks and herds—a considerable number of livestock—on the first night of what we now know as Passover, with their kneading bowls with the unbaked, unleavened dough on their shoulders.

The first taste of freedom for the Israelites—now the fledgling nation of Israel—after spending upwards of four hundred years in Egypt, was spent traipsing from Goshen, which was in the Rameses region in Egypt, to their first encampment at Succoth, which is a Hebrew name for booths or tents. In Succoth the Israelites baked the unleavened dough into cakes of unleavened bread, thus Passover became established as a seven-day festival of Unleavened Bread.

> (A fact that is not widely recognized is that God Almighty brought the Israelites out of Egypt **in order that He might dwell among them:**—
>
> *They will know that I am the* Lord *their God, who brought them out of Egypt **so that** I might dwell among them* (Exodus 29:46).
>
> It is understandable that the Lord God became so furious with Israel when they habitually treated Him, the Lord God Almighty, with such rebellious disrespect.)

The lamb, which all the Israelites were to eat on that night of the first Passover, was to be unblemished and killed on the fourteenth day of the Hebrew month Aviv, which God Almighty had now declared to be the first month of the Hebrew year. The month of *Aviv* was later changed to *Nisan* (Nehemiah 2:1), but it was on this very day, some one thousand three hundred years later, that Yeshua (Jesus) was crucified, and Yeshua (Jesus), the *only begotten Son* of God Almighty, was without sin—he was the unblemished sacrificial **Lamb of God**. Passover night is celebrated each year as a commemoration of when the Israelites came out of Egypt.

Of course, religious Jews today hide this fact that Yeshua (Jesus) was crucified on the fourteenth day of *Nisan*, formerly *Aviv*, and even celebrate the first day of the Hebrew year as being on the first day of the seventh Hebrew month of *Tishrei*, which usually falls in September and October in the Gregorian calendar that most of the world uses.

While the Israelites were camped at Succoth God Almighty told Moses to sanctify (consecrate) every firstborn of man and animal to Him. The LORD God Almighty had killed all the firstborn of man and animal in Egypt, therefore all the firstborn of man and animal among the Israelites—everything that opened the womb—now belonged to Him.

The Israelites were to observe the Passover throughout their generations and on that day they were to tell their sons: —

This is done because of what the LORD God Almighty did for us when we came up from Egypt, with a powerful hand He brought us out of Egypt, from the

house of slavery. And when Pharaoh was stubborn about letting us go, the LORD killed every firstborn in the land of Egypt, both the firstborn of man and the firstborn of animal. Therefore we keep this ordinance at its appointed time from year to year
(Exodus 13:14–15).

After Pharaoh had let the Israelites go, God Almighty did not take them by way of the land of the Philistines, although that was shorter; because He thought, "If the Israelites face war, they may want to return to Egypt." So God Almighty took them by the long route, by way of the wilderness toward the Red Sea. The children of Israel went up out of the land of Egypt in military ranks prepared for battle and Moses fulfilled a solemn oath that he had made with Joseph and took his bones with them. Joseph had made the Israelites swear, saying, "God Almighty will surely visit you, and then you must carry my bones with you from here."

The Israelites set out from their encampment at Succoth, and camped next at Etham, on the edge of the wilderness. God Almighty went before them in a pillar of cloud by day, to show them the way, and in a pillar of fire by night, to provide them with light, so the children of Israel could travel by day and by night. Neither the pillar of cloud by day nor the pillar of fire by night ever left its place in front of them (Exodus 13:17–22).

God Almighty spoke to Moses, saying: "Speak to the children of Israel, tell them to turn and make camp before Pi Hahiroth, between Migdol and the sea, opposite Baal Zephon; you will camp facing it by the sea, because Pharaoh will surely say of the Israelites, 'They are wandering in the land, confused; the wilderness has closed them in.' I will once more harden Pharaoh's heart, and he will give chase and I will obtain glory over Pharaoh and his army, and the Egyptians will know that I am the Lord God Almighty." And so they did.

When the king of Egypt was told that the Israelites had left the country, Pharaoh and his servants changed their minds toward Israel and said, "What is this thing that we have done, that we have let Israel go out from serving us?" So Pharaoh had his chariot made ready and took his whole army with him; he also took six hundred chosen chariots and all the other chariots of Egypt with officers over each of them. And God Almighty hardened the heart of Pharaoh and he pursued the children of Israel as they confidently went out.

The Egyptians chased after the children of Israel, all Pharaoh's horses and chariots, his chariot drivers and his army; they overtook the Israelites encamped by the sea, by Pi-hahiroth, opposite Baal-zephon.

As Pharaoh and his army drew near, the Israelites looked back, and saw the Egyptians advancing on them. The Israelites cried out fearfully to the Lord, and said to Moses, "Was it because there were no graves in Egypt that you have brought us here to die in the desert wilderness? What have you done to us, taking us out of Egypt? Is this not what we told you in Egypt, 'Let us alone and let us serve the Egyptians'? For it would have been better for us to serve the Egyptians than to die here in the desert." Moses said to the people, "Do not be afraid, stand firm, and see the deliverance that God Almighty will accomplish for you today; for the Egyptians whom you see today you will not see again. The Lord God Almighty will fight for you; you have only to remain calm."

Catch us if you can

Then the LORD spoke to Moses, "Why are the people crying out to Me? Tell them to to move on. Raise your staff and stretch it out over the sea and divide it, then the Israelites can go through the sea on dry ground. I will harden the hearts of the Egyptians so that they will pursue the children of Israel and follow them into the sea; and I will obtain honor for Myself over Pharaoh, over his army, his chariots, and his chariot drivers. The Egyptians will know that I am the LORD God Almighty when I have gained honor for Myself over Pharaoh and his army."

Now the angel of the LORD, who was going before the great multitude of the children of Israel, moved and went behind the camp, and the pillar of cloud also moved from before them and then stood behind them, coming between the army of Egypt and the children of Israel. And there was the pillar of cloud and the darkness; it lit up the night without one army coming near the other all night.

Then Moses stretched out his staff over the sea and the LORD God Almighty drove the sea back by a strong east wind all night, turning the seabed into dry land. The waters were divided, forming a road through the sea, and the Israelites went into the sea on dry ground; the waters forming a wall for them on the right and on the left. The Egyptians chased after the Israelites and went into the sea after them, all of Pharaoh's army, his horses, his chariots, and his chariot drivers. At the morning watch the LORD God Almighty, in the pillar of fire and cloud, looked down upon the Egyptian army and threw it into a confused panic. The LORD God Almighty jammed their chariot wheels so that they swerved and turned with difficulty. The Egyptians said, "Let us flee, for the LORD, the God of Israel, is fighting against us."

Then the Lord God Almighty said to Moses, "Stretch out your staff over the sea so that the water will come back upon the Egyptians, upon their chariots and their horsemen." So Moses stretched out his staff over the sea, and at dawn it returned to its normal course. As the Egyptians fled, the Lord God drew them into the midst of the sea and the waters returned and covered the chariots and the horsemen. Of all the multitude of Pharaoh's army that had followed the children of Israel into the sea, not one of them remained. The Israelites had walked on dry ground through the sea, with the waters forming walls on the right and on the left.

That was how God Almighty saved Israel from the Egyptians that day. When the children of Israel saw the Egyptians dead on the seashore they knew of a certainty that they were then truly free, their oppressors were now dead and could oppress them no more. The Israelites broke out in spontaneous songs about God Almighty drowning the entire Egyptian army, all its horses and all its chariots in the sea. Aaron's sister, Miriam, with tambourine in hand led all the women with tambourines in singing and dancing. They sang:—

"Sing to the Lord, for he has triumphed gloriously; horse and rider He has thrown into the sea"
(Exodus 15:21).

Israel had seen the awesome works of power the Lord God had done against the Egyptians, so they feared Him and believed in Him, and in Moses His servant.

Out of the frying pan and into the fire

Then Moses ordered Israel to set out from the Red Sea, and they went into the wilderness of Shur. They walked three days into the wilderness and found no water. When they came to Marah (מרה), they could not drink the water because it was bitter, which is why it was called Marah (מרים – "bitter"). Israel complained against Moses, saying, "What will we drink?"

> *Now when the people complained in the hearing of the* LORD *God Almighty about their misfortunes, and when the* LORD *heard it, His anger was kindled, and the fire of the* LORD *God Almighty burned among them and consumed some outlying parts of the camp. Then the people cried out to Moses, and Moses prayed to the* LORD, *and the fire died down. So the name of that place was called Taberah (שברעה — burning), because the fire of the* LORD *burned among them* (Numbers 11:1–3).

(It took only three days of freedom before Israel began to complain. A chronic complainer today is called a *kvetch* in Israel, and the late Israeli diplomat Abba Eban once said that Israelis are as addicted to *kvetching* as they are to eating. The children of Israel came out from Egypt with reverence for God Almighty but had very little trust in the LORD; they never learned from the burning experience at Marah. Israel undertook a lot more complaining during its trek to the land of Canaan, and the complaints were to take the lives of thousands by the hand of God Almighty.)

Moses cried out to the LORD concerning the lack of sweet water; and the LORD showed him a piece of wood; Moses threw it into the water, and the water became sweet (Exodus 15:22–25).

> (Those who follow Yeshua (Jesus) find that putting the cross of Yeshua (Jesus) into a stressful situation also makes the situation — and consequently life — sweeter.)

The Israelites came to Elim, where there were twelve springs of water and seventy palm trees; and they camped there by the water.

Then the children of Israel broke camp and set out from Elim and came to the wilderness of Sin, which is between Elim and Sinai. Then the whole multitude of Israel did what it was really good at, it complained. Israel complained against Moses and Aaron and complained about the wilderness. The Israelites said to Moses and Aaron, "It would have been better for us had we died by the hand of the LORD God Almighty in Egypt; where we sat by pots of meat and ate our fill of bread. You have brought us into this desert wilderness to kill us with hunger."

So God Almighty said to Moses, "I am going to rain down bread from heaven, and each day the people will go out and gather enough for that day. On the sixth day, when they prepare what they collect, it will be twice as much as they gathered on other days." So Moses and Aaron said to all Israel, "In the morning you will see the glory of the LORD God Almighty, because He has heard your complaining against Him. For what are we, that you complain against us?" Your complaining is not against us but against the LORD."

Out of the frying pan and into the fire

At that time Moses said to Aaron, "Tell the whole congregation, 'Draw near to the LORD, He has heard your complaining.'" As Aaron spoke to the congregation they looked toward the wilderness and the glory of the LORD God Almighty appeared in the cloud. God spoke to Moses and said, "I have heard the *kvetching* of the Israelites; say to them, 'At twilight you will eat meat, and in the morning you will eat your fill of bread; then you will know that I am the LORD God of Israel.'"

In the evening, quails came and thickly covered the ground in the camp; and in the morning there was a layer of dew around the camp. When the layer of dew lifted, there on the surface of the wilderness was a fine, flaky substance on the ground, as fine as frost. When the Israelites saw it, they said to one another, "What is it?" because they did not know what it was. Moses said to them, "It is the bread that the LORD God Almighty has given you to eat." The children of Israel called this bread manna (מן), it looked like white coriander seed and the taste was like wafers made with honey. Moses said "This is what the LORD God Almighty has commanded: 'Gather as much of it as each of you needs, an omer—(two quarts / two liters)—to a person according to the number of persons in their tents.'" Israel did so, some gathering more, some gathering less, but when they measured it with an omer those who gathered much had nothing left over, and those who gathered only a little had no lack. The Israelites gathered as much as each of them needed, and Moses said to them, "Let no one leave any of it over until morning." However, they did not all listen to Moses; some left part of it until morning, and it bred worms and became foul and Moses was angry with them. Every morning they gathered as much manna as they needed; but when the sun grew hot, it melted.

On the sixth day they collected twice as much, two omers apiece. When all the congregation leaders came and told Moses, he said to them, "This is what the Lord God of Israel has commanded: 'Tomorrow is a day of solemn rest, a holy sabbath to the Lord God; bake what you want and boil what you want, and everything that is left over you will keep until morning.'" So they put it aside until morning, as Moses had commanded them; and it did not become foul, and there were no worms in it. Moses said, "Eat it today, for today is a sabbath to the Lord God of Israel; today you will not find any in the field. Six days you will collect it, but on the seventh day, which is a sabbath, there will not be any."

However, it happened that some Israelites went out on the seventh day to gather manna as usual, but they found none. Then the Lord God said to Moses, "How long will they refuse to keep my commands and instructions? Remember, the Lord God has given you the Sabbath and that is why on the sixth day He gives you enough manna for two days. You are to remain where you are on the seventh day, no one is to go out." So the people rested on the seventh day.

Moses said, "This is what the Lord God of Israel has commanded: 'Let an omer of manna be kept throughout your generations, so that they may see the food with which the Lord God fed you in the wilderness, when He brought you out of Egypt.'" And Moses said to Aaron, "Take a jar, and put an omer of manna in it, and place it before the Lord; it is to be kept throughout the generations of Israel." As the Lord God commanded Moses, so Aaron did, later he would place it in the Ark with the covenant, for safekeeping. The children of Israel ate manna for forty

Out of the frying pan and into the fire 151

years, they ate it during their forced wandering in the wilderness; they ate manna every day until they came to the border of Canaan (Exodus 16:1–35).

From the wilderness of Sin Israel journeyed by stages, as the LORD God of Israel commanded. They camped at Rephidim, but there was no water for the people to drink and they quarreled with Moses, they said, "Give us water to drink." So Moses said to them, "Why do you quarrel with me? Why do you test the LORD God?" However, the people thirsted for water and they complained, saying to Moses, "Why did you bring us out of Egypt, to kill us and our children and livestock with thirst?" So Moses cried out to the LORD God of Israel, "What will I do with this people? They are nearly ready to stone me." So the LORD said to Moses, "Go on ahead of the people and take some of the elders with you; take your staff with which you struck the Nile. I will be standing before you on the rock at Horeb. Strike the rock with your staff and water will come out of it, so that the people may drink." Moses did so, in plain view of the elders of Israel. Moses called the place Massah (מסה – *test*) and Meribah (מריבה – *quarrel*), because Israel quarreled and tested the LORD God of Israel.

At Rephidim, Amalek came and fought with Israel, which was something the LORD God of Israel never forgave; and He vowed that Amalek would have war with Him from generation to generation. Its attack against Israel cost Amalek dearly; ultimately it brought about Amalek's obliteration from the pages of history.

At that time Moses said to Joshua, "Choose some men and go, fight with Amalek. Tomorrow I will stand on the top of the hill with the staff of God Almighty in my hand." So Joshua did as Moses said, and fought with Amalek, while Moses, Aaron, and Hur went up to the top of the hill. Whenever Moses held up his hand, Israel proved more powerful; and whenever he lowered his hand, Amalek prevailed. When Moses' hands grew weary, they took a stone and placed it under him for him to sit on. Aaron and Hur then held up the hands of Moses, Aaron on one side, and Hur on the other; so his hands were steady until the setting of the sun. Joshua overwhelmed Amalek with the sword in the battle (Exodus 17:1–13).

> *Then the LORD God said to Moses, "Write this as a memorial in a book and recite it in the ears of Joshua, that I will utterly blot out the memory of Amalek from under heaven"* (Exodus 17:14).

Moses' father-in-law, Jethro (aka Reuel), the priest of Midian, had heard of all the LORD had done for Moses and for the people of Israel, and he had also heard how the LORD God had brought Israel out of Egypt. Moses had sent his wife Zipporah home, now Jethro brought her back, along with her two sons. The name of the first son was Gershom (*"stranger there,"* for Moses had been a stranger in a foreign land), and the name of the other was Eliezer (*"God is my help,"* for the LORD God had delivered Moses from the hand of Pharaoh).

Jethro, the father-in-law of Moses, came into the wilderness where Moses was encamped and brought Moses' sons and wife to him. Moses then told his father-in-law all that the LORD God had done to Pharaoh and to the Egyptians on Israel's behalf. He also told Jethro of all the misfortunes that had been endured on the way, and how the LORD God of Israel had delivered them. Jethro was delighted to hear of all the good the LORD had done for Israel, in delivering them from the Egyptians.

The following day Moses sat as judge for the congregation, and the people stood around him from early morning until the going down of the sun at evening. When Jethro saw all that Moses was doing, he said, "What is this that you are doing for the people? Why do you sit alone, while all the people stand around you all day long?" Moses said to his father-in-law, "When they have a dispute, they come to me and I decide between one person and another, and I make known to them the instructions of God Almighty." Jethro said to Moses, "What you are doing is not good. You will certainly wear yourself out, both you and these people with you. The task is too much for you, you cannot do this alone. Now listen to your father-in-law! You should represent the people before God Almighty and you should bring their cases before Him and teach them His instructions and show them the way they are to go and the things they are to do. But find able men from among all the people, men who fear the LORD God, are trustworthy, and who reject dishonesty. Set those men as officers over thousands, hundreds, fifties and tens and let them sit as judges for the people. Let them bring every important case to you, but they should decide every insignificant case themselves. It will be easier for you and they will help bear the burden with you If you do this you will be able to cope, and all these people will go in peace to their homes."

So Moses listened to his father-in-law and did what he had advised. Moses chose capable men from among the people and appointed them over all the people, as officers over thousands, hundreds, fifties, and tens. These men judged the minor cases of the congregation. but the important cases they brought to Moses. Then Jethro left Moses and went to his own country (Exodus 18:1–27).

On the third full moon after Israel had left the land of Egypt, on that very day, Israel came into the wilderness of Sinai. The Israelites had journeyed from Rephidim, entered the wilderness of Sinai and was encamped in front of the mountain of God. Then Moses went up the mountain to God Almighty, who had called Moses to Himself from the mountain, saying, "This is what you will say to the house of Jacob. Say to the children of Israel":—

You have seen what I did to the Egyptians, and how I bore you on eagles' wings and brought you to myself. Now therefore, if you obey my voice and keep my covenant, you will be my treasured possession out of all the peoples. Indeed, the whole earth is mine, but you will be for me a priestly kingdom and a holy nation. These are the words that you will speak to the Israelites (Exodus 19:4–6).

So Moses came down from the mountain, called for the elders of Israel, and told them all that the LORD God of Israel had commanded. The people all answered as one: "Everything the LORD God has said we will do." Moses reported these words to God Almighty. Then the LORD God said to Moses:—

I am going to come to you in a dense cloud, in order that the people may hear when I speak with you and they will put their trust in you for ever (Exodus 19:9).

When Moses had told the LORD the words of the people, He said to Moses: "Go to the people and consecrate them today and tomorrow. Have them wash their clothes and prepare for the third day, because on the third day I will come down upon Mount Sinai in the sight of all the people. You will set boundaries all around, and say, 'Be careful not to go onto the mountain or to touch even the edge of it. Anyone who touches the mountain will be put to death. They must be stoned or shot through with arrows, whether animal or human, they cannot live.' When the trumpet sounds a long blast, the people may approach the mountain." So Moses went down from the mountain again to the people. He consecrated them, and they washed their clothes. Moses said to all the people, "Prepare for the third day; do not have sex with your wives."

On the morning of the third day there were thunders and lightnings and a thick cloud on the mountain. A very loud trumpet blast sounded so that all the people in the camp trembled. Then Moses brought the people out of the camp to meet God Almighty, and they stood at the foot of the mountain. Now Mount Sinai was cloaked in smoke because the LORD God of Israel had descended upon it in fire. Smoke went up like the smoke of a great furnace and the entire mountain violently shook and trembled. As the sound of the trumpet grew louder and louder, Moses would speak and the LORD God answered him in thunder.

The LORD God came down on Mount Sinai, on the top of the mountain, and the LORD called Moses to the top of the mountain, and Moses went up to Him again.

Then God Almighty said to Moses, "Go down and warn the people not to break through to the LORD to look, because many of them will die. Even the priests who approach the LORD God must consecrate themselves or I will break out against them." Moses said to the LORD, "The people are not permitted to come up Mount Sinai; for you warned us, saying, 'Set boundaries around the mountain and consecrate it.'" Then God Almighty said to Moses, "Go down again, and come back up, bringing Aaron with you; but do not let the priests or the people force themselves through to come up to the LORD; because I will break out against them." So Moses went down to the people and told them what God Almighty had said.

Moses was then told by the LORD God that He would write His covenant—His commandments—on two tablets of stone and that Israel was to rigorously observe this covenant throughout all generations. Then God Almighty said to Moses, "Come up to Me on the mountain, and wait there and I will give you the tablets of stone, with the law and the commandment, which I have written for their instruction." So Moses set out with his assistant Joshua, and they went up into the mountain of God. Moses said to the elders, "Wait here for us, until we come to you; Aaron and Hur are with you, whomsoever has a dispute may go to them."

So Moses went up on the mountain, and the cloud covered the mountain. The glory of the LORD God Almighty settled on Mount Sinai, and the cloud covered it for six days; on the seventh day the LORD God called to Moses out of the cloud. (The manifestation of the glory of the LORD was like a consuming fire on the top of the mountain in the sight of all the people of Israel.) Moses entered the cloud and went up on the mountain. Moses remained on the mountain for forty days and forty nights, he neither ate bread nor drank water. When God Almighty finished speaking with Moses on Mount Sinai, He gave him two tablets of stone, the Ten Commandments—the words of the covenant—written with the finger of God (Exodus 24:3–15).

Then the unthinkable happened:—

When the Israelites saw that Moses delayed coming down from the mountain, they assembled together, came to Aaron and said: "Come, make us a god who will go before us. We do not know what has become of this Moses, the man who brought us up out of the land of Egypt," and so Aaron said to them, "Take off the gold rings that are in the ears of your wives, your sons, and your daughters, and bring them to me." So the people took off the rings that were in their ears and gave them to Aaron. He received their gold, formed it in a mold and fashioned it with an engraving tool and made it into a golden calf. And the people said, "This is your god, O Israel, who brought you up out of the land of Egypt!" (Exodus 32:1–4).

Moses went down the mountain with Joshua his assistant, and when they neared the camp of the Israelites they heard the shouting and singing of the people. And when they saw the golden calf and the people dancing the anger of Moses burned fiercely and he threw the tablets from his hands and shattered them at the foot of the mountain. Then he took the calf that Aaron had made, burnt it with fire, ground it to dust and scattered it on the surface of the water and made the people drink it, but Aaron had let the people get out of control and their enemies were ridiculing them. Then Moses said, "Whoever is on the LORD's side come to me," and the Levites gathered to him. Moses then said, this is what the LORD God of Israel, the Almighty says:—

Let each man fasten his sword to his side and go back and forth from entrance to entrance throughout the camp, and each one kill his brother, his friend, and his neighbor (Exodus 32:27)

The Levites did what Moses commanded and about three thousand children of Israel died that day. God Almighty then told Moses to cut two more tablets of stone, like those that were shattered, and come back up the mountain where He would write the ten words afresh on the tablets. God Almighty was of a mind to kill all the children of Israel over the golden calf incident, but Moses earnestly pleaded for them, and prevailed; however, the Lord sent a plague among the people, because they had made the calf—the one which Aaron made.

Moses came down from the mountain again, carrying the new tablets which bore the ten words written with the finger of God Almighty. And those ten words were:—

I am the Lord your God, who brought you out of the land of Egypt, out of the house of slavery and bondage; you will have no other gods before me.

You will not make for yourself an idol, whether in the form of anything that is in heaven above, or that is on the earth beneath, or that is in the water under the earth. You will not bow down to them or worship them; for I the Lord your God am a jealous God, punishing children for the iniquity of parents, to the third and the fourth generation of those who reject me, but showing steadfast love to the thousandth generation of those who love me and keep my commandments.

You will not make wrongful use of the name of the Lord your God, for the Lord will not absolve anyone who misuses his name.

Remember the sabbath day, and keep it holy. Six days you will labor and do all your work. But the seventh day is a sabbath to the Lord your God; you will not do any work—you, your son or your daughter, your male or female slave, your livestock, or the alien resident in your towns. For in six days the Lord made heaven and earth, the sea, and all that is in them, but

> rested the seventh day; therefore the LORD blessed the sabbath day and consecrated it.
>
> Honor your father and your mother, so that your days may be long in the land that the LORD your God is giving you.
>
> You shall not murder.
>
> You shall not commit adultery.
>
> You shall not steal.
>
> You shall not bear false witness against your neighbor.
>
> You shall not covet your neighbor's house; you shall not covet your neighbor's wife, or male or female slave, or ox, or donkey, or anything that belongs to your neighbor (Exodus 20:2–17).

At that time God Almighty said to all the children of Israel:—

> So now, O Israel, what does the LORD your God require of you? Only to fear the LORD your God, to walk in all His ways, to love Him, to serve the LORD your God with all your heart and with all your soul, and to keep the commandments of the LORD your God and His decrees that I am commanding you today, for your own good (Deuteronomy 10:12–13).

God Almighty was to double down on the keeping of His commandments; it came down to a matter of life and death:—

> You will therefore keep my statutes and my rules; if a person does them, he will live by them: I am the LORD
> (Leviticus 18:5).

The Ten Commandments have been the guide of Western civilizations for centuries but, as America implodes and destroys itself in the new millennium, godlessness takes reign and copies of the Ten Commandments placed on courthouses, schools and other public buildings are being removed in the new "Woke" culture.

Thomas Macaulay, the British historian who died in 1861 on the eve of the American Civil War, wrote of the United States:

> Your republic will be fearfully plundered and laid waste by barbarians in the twentieth century as the Roman Empire was in the fifth, with this difference: that the Huns and Vandals will have been engendered within your own country, by your own institutions.

At this time of writing America's own engendered huns and vandals are busily laying waste to the country.

From slavery to bondage

In addition to the Ten Commandments various laws, statutes and regulations pertaining to sacrifices, foods, social behavior *et al* were added by God Almighty, and Rabbis have augmented the law of Moses while conniving ways to get around a number of the laws that intrude upon their own personal lives. By the third century C.E. Jewish tradition had acknowledged six hundred and thirteen *mitzvoth* (commandments) which Jews must observe; some carrying the death penalty if they are broken. However, *"whoever keeps the whole law and yet stumbles at just one point is guilty of breaking all of it"* (James 2:10); and: —

> *we know that whatever the Law says, it speaks to those who are under the Law, so that every mouth may be silenced, and the whole world may be held accountable to God. For no one will be justified in his sight by deeds prescribed by the Law, for through the Law comes the consciousness of sin*
> (Romans 3:19–20).

Therefore there is no escape from the requirements of the Law *"for all have sinned and fall short of the glory of God"* (Romans 3:23). The Law of Moses is a double-edged sword: keep the Law and live eternally; break the Law and die. God Almighty admits that the Law of Moses could not be kept when He says: *"I gave them statutes that were not good and rules by which they could not live"* (Ezekiel 20:25). But God Almighty already had the answer to the dilemma even before time began; and Yeshua (Jesus), the *unblemished Lamb of God "was foreordained before the foundation of the world, but was revealed in these last days for you"* (1Peter 1:20). The coming of Yeshua (Jesus) is foretold throughout the Scriptures, beginning at Genesis 3:15, but the Rabbis and Jewish sages have hidden it from the Jewish people.

If the six hundred and thirteen mitzvoth (commandments) were not enough, the Rabbis also brought in the Oral Law, which is a legal commentary on both the Ten Commandments and the Law of Moses, and which speaks for all the commandments, statutes and legal interpretations that were not recorded in the *Torah* (the five books of Moses — the first five books of the Bible). The Oral Law explains how each commandment and statute is to be carried out and contains the Sabbath rituals such as the lighting of candles, the prayers and blessings (*kiddish*) over the wine and bread at the meal which ushers in the Sabbath and other holy days. It is therefore understandable why Yeshua (Jesus) would say, concerning the Jews: *"It is **written in your law**..."* (John 8:17 and 10:34) and, *"this is to fulfill **what is written in their Law**..."* (John 15:25). Yeshua (Jesus) differentiated between God Almighty's law and the preponderance of Jewish rabbinical law.

The Israelites came out of slavery and bondage to the Egyptians only to be chained and shackled once again, this time to the Rabbinical interpretation of the Law of Moses, which, for the descendants of Jacob, was rather like "out of the frying pan and into the fire." However, God Almighty shows us in His Word that everything was temporary –the Law, the tabernacle in the wilderness, the Temple – were merely *"shadows of the good things to come"* (Hebrews 8:5, 10:1), and as we progress with this book the whole ingenious plan of God Almighty will become clear.

When the children of Israel witnessed the events at Mount Sinai—the thunder, the lightning, the sound of the trumpet, and the mountain itself smoking—they were afraid and trembled with fear and kept their distance. The people had seen for themselves that God Almighty spoke with them from heaven and said to Moses, "You speak to us, and we will listen; but do not let God Almighty speak to us, or we will die." So Moses said to the children of Israel, "Do not be afraid; for God Almighty has come only to test you and to put the fear of Him into you so that you will not sin." The people continued to stand at a distance, but Moses drew near to the thick darkness where God Almighty was and received further ordinances concerning sacrifices and male and female slaves, and then went down again to the encampment at the foot of the mountain and told the people all the words of the Lord and all the ordinances. And with one voice all the people answered Moses and said, "All that the Lord God has spoken we will do, and we will be obedient," and Moses wrote down in a book all the words of God Almighty.

Moses rose early in the morning and built an altar at the foot of the mountain and set up twelve pillars representing the twelve tribes. After that Moses then sent young men from the children of Israel and they offered burnt offerings and sacrificed oxen as peace offerings to the Lord God Almighty. And Moses took half of the blood from the offerings and splashed it against the altar and then read the book of the covenant to the people. After he had closed the book of the covenant Moses took the rest of the blood and splashed it on the people, while saying, "This is the blood of the covenant that God Almighty has made with you in accordance with all these words written in this book.

Then the Lord God said to Moses, "Come up, you and Aaron, Nadab, and Abihu, and bring seventy of the elders of Israel and worship at a distance. You alone will come near Me; but the others will not come near, and the people of Israel will not come up the mountain." Then Moses and Aaron, Nadab, and Abihu, and seventy of the elders of Israel went up the mountain, and they saw the LORD God of Israel. Under His feet there was something like a pavement of sapphire stone, as blue as the sky itself. God Almighty did not lay his hand on the chief men of Israel. They saw God and they ate and drank (Exodus 21:22–24:1–11).

> (John 1:18: *"No one has ever seen God; the only God, who is at the Father's side, he has made Him known."* This is not in conflict with Exodus 24:11. What they actually saw at the top of Mount Sinai was a 'form', a similitude or 'likeness' of God Almighty, not His actual self. Compare Exodus 24:11 with Exodus 33:20 where God Almighty shows Moses His glory. God says to Moses:—
>> *"But you cannot see my face, for no man can see me and live."* And the LORD said, *"Behold, there is a place by me where you will stand on the rock, and while my glory passes by I will put you in a cleft of the rock, and I will cover you with my hand until I have passed by. Then I will take away my hand, and you will see my back, but my face will not be seen"*
>> (Exodus 33:20.)

Tabernacle in the Wilderness

At that time God Almighty gave Moses instructions for building a tabernacle (tabernacle means "tent"), a holy sanctuary, in the wilderness. The tabernacle was to be a work of art. God Almighty told Moses to take an offering from the people, from those whose hearts were zealous for giving to the project. Moses was told to receive from the children of Israel: bronze, gold and silver, blue, purple, and crimson yarns and fine linen, goats' hair, tanned rams' skins, fine leather, acacia wood, oil for lamps, spices for anointing oil and for fragrant incense, onyx stones and gems to be set in an ephod (a sleeveless garment worn by Israel's priests) and for a breastpiece for Aaron (made from the same material as the ephod and having twelve precious gems in four rows and engraved with the names of the twelve tribes of Israel, firmly fixed and hung from the shoulders of the ephod of Aaron with cords of woven gold going through gold rings). And God Almighty said to Moses:—

> *Have the Israelites make me a sanctuary exactly as I will show you, **in order that I may dwell among them**. They will make it according to all that I show you concerning the pattern of the tabernacle and its furniture"* (Exodus 25:1–9).

Then the LORD God Almighty told Moses of all that he needed to make for the tabernacle, giving measurements for each item and of what material it was to be made. The list began with the Ark, which would later contain the tablets of stone on which God Almighty had written the covenant (the ten commandments); a jar containing an omer of manna; and Aaron's rod which had sprouted buds and bore almonds. The Ark was to be of acacia wood, two and a half cubits long (a cubit was about eighteen inches—forty-four centimeters), a width of one and a half cubits, and one and a half cubits high. It was to be overlaid with pure gold inside and out. It was to have a gold molding and four rings of cast gold for holding carrying poles, which were also to be made of acacia wood and overlaid with gold and they were never to be removed from the Ark. Next:—

> *You will make a mercy seat of pure gold; two and a half cubits will be its length, and a cubit and a half its width. You will make two cherubim of gold; you will make them of hammered work, at the two ends of the mercy seat. Make one cherub at the one end, and one cherub at the other; the cherubim will be of one piece with the mercy seat you will make the cherubim at its two ends. The cherubim will spread out their wings above, overshadowing the mercy seat. They will face one another; and the faces of the cherubim will be toward the mercy seat. You will put the mercy seat on the top of the ark; and in the ark you will put the covenant that I will give you. There I will meet with you, and from above the mercy seat, from between the two cherubim that are on the ark of the covenant, I will speak all my commands for the children of Israel.*
>
> *You will make a table of acacia wood, two cubits long, one cubit wide, and a cubit and a half high. You will overlay it with gold, and make a molding with its rim a handbreadth wide of gold all around the rim. You will make for it four rings of gold, and fasten the rings to the four corners at its four legs. The rings that hold the poles used for carrying the table will*

be close to the rim. You will make the poles of acacia wood, and overlay them with gold, and the table will be carried with these. You will make its plates and dishes for incense, and its flagons and bowls with which to pour drink offerings; you will make them of pure gold. And you will set the bread of the Presence on the table before Me always.

You will make a lampstand of pure gold. The base and the shaft of the lampstand will be made of hammered work; its cups, its calyxes, and its petals will be of one piece with it; and there will be six branches going out of its sides, three branches of the lampstand out of one side of it and three branches of the lampstand out of the other side of it; three cups shaped like almond blossoms, each with calyx and petals, on one branch, and three cups shaped like almond blossoms, each with calyx and petals, on the other branch—so for the six branches going out of the lampstand. On the lampstand itself there will be four cups shaped like almond blossoms, each with its calyxes and petals. There will be a calyx of one piece with it under the first pair of branches, a calyx of one piece with it under the next pair of branches, and a calyx of one piece with it under the last pair of branches—so for the six branches that go out of the lampstand. Their calyxes and their branches will be of one piece with it, the whole of it one hammered piece of pure gold. You will make the seven lamps for it; and the lamps will be set up so as to give light on the space in front of it. Its snuffers and trays will be of pure gold. It, and all these utensils, will be made from a talent of pure gold. And see that you make them according to the pattern for them, which is being shown you on the mountain (Exodus 25:17–40). — (A biblical talent of gold weighed seventy-five pounds — thirty-five kilograms.)

Then God Almighty said to Moses:—
You will make the tabernacle with ten curtains of fine twisted linen, and blue, purple, and crimson yarns; you will make them with cherubim skillfully worked into them. The length of each curtain will be twenty-eight cubits, and the width of each curtain four cubits; all the curtains will be the same size. Five curtains will be joined together; and the other five will be joined together. You will make loops of blue on the edge of the outermost curtain in the first set; and likewise you will make loops on the edge of the outermost curtain in the second set. You will make fifty loops on the one curtain, and you will make fifty loops on the edge of the curtain that is in the second set; the loops will be opposite one another. You will make fifty gold clasps and join the curtains together with them so that the tabernacle will be one unit.

You will also make curtains of goats' hair for a tent over the tabernacle; you will make eleven curtains. The length of each curtain will be thirty cubits and its width four cubits; all eleven curtains will be the same size. You will join five curtains together and six curtains together; the sixth curtain you will double over at the front of the tent. You will make fifty loops on the edge of the outermost curtain in one set, and fifty loops on the edge of the curtain that is outermost in the second set.

You will make fifty clasps of bronze and put the clasps into the loops, and join the tent together, so that it may be one unit. The half curtain that remains will hang over the back of the tabernacle. The cubit on the one side, and the cubit on the other side, of what remains in the length of the curtains of the tent, will hang over each side of the tabernacle, to cover it. You will make for the tent a covering of tanned rams' skins dyed red and an outer covering of goatskins.

You will make upright frames of acacia wood for the tabernacle. Ten cubits will be the length of a frame, and a cubit and a half the width. There will be two pegs in each frame to fit the frames together; you will make these for all the frames of the tabernacle. You will make twenty frames for the south side and twenty frames for the north side and six frames for the rear of the tabernacle. Under each frame you will make bases of silver for the two pegs of the frames. You will make two frames for corners of the tabernacle in the rear; they will be separate beneath, but joined at the top at the first ring. It will be the same for both of them, they will form the two corners. There will be eight frames with their sixteen bases of silver, two bases under the first frame, and two bases under the next frame.

You will make bars of acacia wood, five for the frames of the one side of the tabernacle, and five for the frames of the other side of the tabernacle, and five bars for the frames of the side of the tabernacle at the rear westward. The middle bar, midway up the frames, will pass through from end to end. You will overlay the frames with gold, and will make their rings of gold to hold the bars; and you will overlay the bars with gold. Then you will erect the tabernacle according to what you were shown on the mountain.

You will make a veil of blue, purple, and crimson yarns, and of fine twisted linen and made with cherubim skillfully worked into it. You will hang it on four pillars of acacia wood overlaid with gold, which will have hooks of gold and rest on four bases of silver. You will hang the veil and bring the ark of the covenant in within the veil; and the veil will separate the Holy place from the Most Holy place. You will put the mercy seat on the ark of the covenant in the Most Holy place. You will put the table outside the veil, and the lampstand on the south side of the tabernacle opposite the table, which will stand on the north side.

You will make a screen for the entrance of the tent, of blue, purple, and crimson yarns, and of fine twisted linen, embroidered with needlework. You will make for the screen five pillars of acacia wood and overlay them with gold; their hooks will be of gold, and you will cast five bases of bronze for them.

You will make the altar of acacia wood, five cubits long and five cubits wide; the altar will be square, and it will be three cubits high. You will make horns for it on its four corners; and the horns will be of one piece with it, and you will overlay the whole altar with bronze. You will make pots for it to receive its ashes, and shovels and basins and forks and firepans; you will make all the utensils of bronze. You will also make for it a grating, a network of bronze, and on the network you will make four rings of bronze at its corners for its carrying poles. You will set it under the ledge of the altar so that the network will extend halfway down the altar. You will make poles of acacia wood for the altar, and overlay them with bronze; the poles will be put through the rings on the two sides of the altar when it is carried. You will make it hollow, with boards. They will be made exactly as you were shown on the mountain.

Tabernacle in the Wilderness   171

You will make the court of the tabernacle. On the south side the court will have hangings of fine twisted linen one hundred cubits long for that side; its twenty pillars and twenty bases will be of bronze, but the pillars' hooks and their bands will be made of silver. The same for its length on the north side, there will be hangings one hundred cubits long, the twenty pillars and the twenty bases will be of bronze, but the hooks of the pillars and their bands will be of silver. The court's width on the west side will be fifty cubits of hangings, with ten pillars and ten bases. The width of the court on the front will be fifty cubits. There will be fifteen cubits of hangings on each side, with three pillars and three bases. For the gate of the court there will be a screen twenty cubits long, of blue, purple, and crimson yarns, and of fine twisted linen, embroidered with the needlework of an embroiderer; it will have four pillars and their four bases. All the pillars of the court will be banded with silver; their hooks will be silver, and their bases bronze. The length of the court will be one hundred cubits, its breadth fifty, and its height will be five cubits, with hangings of fine twisted linen and bases of bronze. All the utensils of the tabernacle and all all the pegs of the court, will be bronze.

You will command the Israelites to bring you pure oil from pressed olives for the lamp, so that light will burn continually. In the tent of meeting, outside the curtain that is before the covenant, Aaron and his sons will tend the lamps from evening to morning before the LORD. It will be a perpetual statute to be observed throughout the generations of the children of Israel.

> (The tabernacle was a splendorous mix of substance and Israeli artisan prowess. It

was a tabernacle, a tent truly worthy of God Almighty, Israel's Maker and King. Gold and silver were in abundance, especially gold (courtesy of the Egyptians) and the profusion of color from its hangings and curtains of crimson, scarlet, purple, blue and its ceiling of rams' skins dyed red. All this handmade beauty, skillful artisan work in wood, tapestry and precious metals was carried out in a desert wasteland where there were no carpentry or metalwork shops. Today its value would be absolutely incalculable.

The veil that separated the Holy Place from the Most Holy place was skillfully woven in blue, scarlet and purple and portrayed cherubim (angels) made of gold thread from finely beaten gold. Within the veil was the Ark of God Almighty, the ark of the covenant, upon which was placed a solid gold mercy seat which formed a second lid to the chest containing the Ten Commandments written with the finger of God Almighty, the written Law of Moses, the jar of manna and Aaron's rod that had budded and brought forth almonds. The mercy seat had an angel (cherub) at each end, beaten out from and in one piece with the mercy seat, their faces faced down toward the mercy seat and their wings overshadowed the mercy seat and Yahweh (יהוה), God Most High, would appear under the angels' wings. In Hebrew, mercy seat is *"the kaporet"* (הכפרת), which means to atone for and cover sins committed. Once a year, on the Day of Atonement (הכפרים יום — Leviticus 23:27–28), known in the West as Yom Kippur, the High Priest would sprinkle blood from a sacrificial lamb on the mercy seat. On this day the LORD (יהוה), Yahweh, would see the blood of the sacrifice and the sins of the people would be atoned for. Now fast forward several centuries to where it becomes personal for all of us. We now see God Almighty's answer to sin, which is Yeshua (Jesus), *the Lamb of God who takes away the sin of the world* (John 1:29): —

> *whom God put forward as a propitiation, a sacrifice of atonement by His blood, to be **received by faith**. This was to show God's righteousness, because in His forbearance He had passed over all sins committed previously* (Romans 3:25).

With the mercy seat being on top of the chest containing the written Law of Moses, the mercy seat effectively hid God's people from the condemning judgments of the Law. The mercy seat shows us that it is only through the offering of blood that the condemnation of the Law can be taken away, and violations of God Almighty's laws covered. Yeshua (Jesus) today performs the functions of the mercy seat for all those who by faith put their trust in him:—

> *We have been delivered from the letter of the law, having died to what we were held by, so that we should be slaves not under the old written code, but in the new life of the Spirit*
>
>   (Romans 7:6.)

God Almighty then said to Moses, "Now bring your brother Aaron and his sons out from among the Israelites to minister to me as priests—Aaron and his sons Nadab, Abihu, Eleazar and Ithamar. You must make **holy** vestments for **splendor** and **beauty** to adorn your brother Aaron. You will speak to all who have ability, all those to whom I have given wisdom and skill, that they make Aaron's vestments to consecrate him for My priesthood. These are the vestments that they will make: a breastpiece, an ephod, a robe, a plaited tunic, a turban, and a sash. When they make these holy vestments for your brother Aaron and his sons they will use gold, blue, purple, and crimson yarns, and fine linen.

They will make the ephod of skillfully worked gold, blue, purple, and crimson yarns, and of fine twisted linen. It will have two shoulder-pieces attached to its two edges, so that it may be joined together. The decorated band on it will be of the same workmanship and materials, of gold, blue, purple and crimson yarns, and fine twisted linen. You will take two onyx stones, and engrave on them the names of the sons of Israel, six of their names on the one stone, and the remaining six names on the other stone, all in the order of their birth. As a gem-cutter engraves signets, so you will engrave the two stones with the names of the sons of Israel; you will mount them in settings of gold filigree. You will set the two stones on the shoulder-pieces of the ephod as stones of remembrance for the sons of Israel. Aaron will bear the names of the sons of Israel before the Lord on his shoulders for remembrance. You will make settings of gold filigree for the stones and two chains of pure gold, twisted like cords, and you will attach the corded chains to the settings.

You will make a breastpiece in skilled work for decisions and judgments; you will make it in the style of the ephod, of gold, blue, purple and crimson yarns, and fine twisted linen. It will be square and doubled, a span (roughly half a cubit) in length and a span in breadth. You will set four rows of stones in it. A row of carnelian, chrysolite, and emerald will be the first row; and in the second row a turquoise, a sapphire and a moonstone. In the third row a jacinth, an agate, and an amethyst; and in the fourth row a beryl, an onyx, and a jasper; they will all be set in gold filigree. There will be twelve stones with names corresponding to the names of the sons of Israel; they will be like signets, each engraved with its name, for the twelve tribes. You will make for the breastpiece chains of pure gold, twisted like cords; and you will make for the breastpiece two rings of gold, and put the two rings on the two edges of the breastpiece. You will put the two cords of gold in the two rings at the edges of the breastpiece; the two ends of the two cords you will attach to the two settings, and so attach it in front to the shoulder-pieces of the ephod. You will make two rings of gold, and put them at the two ends of the breastpiece, on its inside edge next to the ephod. You will make two rings of gold, and attach them in front to the lower part of the two shoulder-pieces of the ephod, at its joining above the decorated band of the ephod. The breastpiece will be bound by its rings to the rings of the ephod with a blue cord, so that it may lie on the decorated band of the ephod, and so that the breastpiece will not come loose from the ephod. So Aaron will bear the names of the sons of Israel in the breastpiece of judgment on his heart when he goes into the holy place, for a continual remembrance before the Lord. In the breastpiece of judgment you will put the Urim and the Thummim, and they will be on Aaron's heart when he goes in before the Lord; thus Aaron will bear the judgment of the Israelites on his heart before the Lord continually.

You will make the robe of the ephod all of blue. It will have an opening for the head, with a woven binding around the opening, like the opening in a coat of mail. On its lower hem you will make pomegranates of blue, purple and crimson yarns, all around the hem, with bells of gold in between—a gold bell and a pomegranate alternating all around the hem of the robe. Aaron will wear it when he ministers, and its sound will be heard when he goes into the holy place before the Lord and when he comes out, so that he does not die.

You will make a shining plate, a crown of pure gold, and engrave on it, like the engraving of a signet, "Holy to the Lord." You will fasten it securely to the front of the turban with a blue cord. It will be on Aaron's forehead, and Aaron will bear any guilt incurred in the holy offerings that the children of Israel consecrate as their holy offerings. The crown will always be on his forehead, in order that the offerings will be accepted by the Lord God Almighty.

You will make the plaited tunic of fine linen, and you will make a turban of fine linen, and you will make a sash embroidered with the needlework of an embroiderer.

Tabernacle in the Wilderness

For Aaron's sons you will make tunics, sashes and head-coverings; you will make them for **glorious, beautiful adornment**. You will put them on your brother Aaron and on his sons with him, and will anoint them and ordain them and consecrate them, so that they may minister to Me as priests. You will make for them linen undergarments to cover their bare flesh and they will reach from waist to thigh. Aaron and his sons must wear them whenever they go into the tent of meeting (aka the tabernacle) and when coming near the altar to serve in the holy place, or else they will bring guilt on themselves and die. This will be a perpetual statute for Aaron and for all his descendants."

(The garments, or vestments, of Aaron (the High Priest) and his sons were designed to be especially glorious, splendid, and beautiful in order that the splendor of Aaron's position as God Almighty's anointed representative could be clearly seen and understood. Only the most wealthy and powerful king would dare to be clothed in such glory and grandeur, and such was Aaron's status. On each of Aaron's ephod shoulder pieces was an onyx gemstone, on one stone was engraved—in birth order—six of the names of the twelve tribes and the remaining six names were engraved on the other stone. The twelve precious stones on the breastpiece, which was for judgments and decisions, were set in gold filigree, and each stone had the name of one of the twelve tribes engraved on it. The Urim and Thummim—Lights and Perfections—

were in a pouch attached to the inside of the breastpiece of judgement. It was via the Urim and Thummim that God Almighty made His decisions and judgments known to Aaron.)

And God Almighty said to Moses, "This is what you must do to Aaron and his sons to consecrate them, so that they may minister to Me as priests. You will take one young bull and two rams without blemish, unleavened bread, unleavened cakes mixed with oil, and unleavened wafers spread with oil. You will make them of choice wheat flour. You will put them in a basket and bring the basket, the bull and the two rams to the entrance of the tent of meeting (aka the tabernacle). You must then bring Aaron and his sons, and wash them with water. Then you will take the holy garments and put on Aaron the tunic and the robe of the ephod, and breastpiece, and gird him with the decorated band of the ephod; and you will then put the turban on his head and put the holy crown on the turban. You must then take the anointing oil and pour it on his head and anoint him. After that you will bring his sons and put tunics on them, and you will gird them with sashes and tie head coverings on them. The priesthood will be theirs by a perpetual statute. You must then ordain Aaron and his sons.

You will bring the bull before the tent of meeting. Aaron and his sons will lay their hands on its head and then you will kill the bull before the Lord at the entrance of the tent of meeting. You must take part of the blood of the bull and put it on the horns of the altar with your finger, and the rest of the blood you must pour out at the base of the altar. You will then take all the fat that covers the entrails, and the lobe of the liver, together with the two kidneys with their fat, and burn them on the altar. The flesh of the bull, its skin and its dung you must burn with fire outside the camp; it is a purification of sin offering.

Then you must take one of the rams, and Aaron and his sons will lay their hands on its head, and you will kill it and splash its blood against all four sides of the altar. Then you will cut the ram into its pieces, wash its entrails and legs, and put them with its pieces and head, and burn the whole ram on the altar. It is a burnt offering to the LORD. It is a pleasing aroma, an offering by fire to the LORD.

You must take the other ram, and Aaron and his sons will lay their hands on its head. You will kill it and take some of its blood and put it on the lobe of Aaron's right ear, and on the right lobes of the ears of his sons, on the thumbs of each of their right hands, and on the big toes of each of their right feet, and splash the rest of the blood against all four sides of the altar. Then you must take some of the blood that is on the altar, and some of the anointing oil, and sprinkle it on Aaron and on his holy garments, and on his sons' holy garments; then he and his garments will be holy, as well as his sons and his sons' holy garments."

> (The anointing of Aaron and his sons points toward the consecration of all Christians—*"called saints"* or holy ones (Romans 1:7)—who truly believe in Yeshua (Jesus). In Isaiah Chapter six the prophet reports that he saw God Almighty sitting on His throne in His heavenly temple, and the train of His robe was filling the house. Six-winged seraphs—angels of the upper hierarchy—were above the throne and were engaged in responsive worship of the

LORD. The seraphim called out to one another, crying. *"Holy, Holy, Holy is the LORD of armies, the whole earth if full of His glory."* And at the sound of these six-winged seraphs the doorposts and threshold of the temple shook and trembled. Isaiah himself cries out:—

> *Woe is me, for I am ruined, because I am a man of unclean lips and I live among a people of unclean lips; for my eyes hav seen the King, the LORD of armies*
>
> (Isaiah 6:5).

Isaiah was saying that in comparison to a Holy LORD God he was a leper, and that he lived among a whole nation of leprous people. If we are real we will understand that we, too, are lepers when matched against a holy and pure God, and that our peoples are also leprous.

Jewish law decreed that lepers had to cover the upper lip and cry out "Unclean! Unclean!"

> *The leprous person who has the disease will wear torn clothes and let the hair of his head hang loose, and he will cover his upper lip and cry out, 'Unclean! Unclean!' He is unclean and all the days he has the disease he is unclean. He is unclean, and he will dwell alone; his dwelling is to be outside the camp* (Leviticus 13:45–46).

Then one of the seraphs, using tongs, brought a burning coal from the alter of God Almighty and touched Isaiah's mouth with it, saying, *"See, this has touched your lips; your iniquity is taken away and your sin atoned for."* Fortunately, we do not need a seraph to touch our mouths withe a burning coal from the altar of God Almighty in order to remove our iniquity and sin. Because Yeshua (Jesus):—

> *washed us from our sins in his own blood and made us a kingdom of priests serving his God and Father, to him be glory and dominion forever and ever. Amen* (Revelation 1:5–6).

Leprosy was a severe disease in Old Testament times just as sin today is a severe disease in modern times; however, lepers in Old Testament times were cleansed in the same way as the priests were anointed:—

> *The priest will slaughter the lamb of the guilt offering and will take some of the blood of the guilt offering, and put it on the lobe of the right ear of the one to be cleansed, and on the thumb of the right hand, and on the big toe of the right foot* (Leviticus 14:25).

> *Some of the oil that is in his hand the priest will put on the lobe of the right ear of the one to be cleansed, and on the thumb of the right hand, and on the big toe of the right foot, on top of the blood of the guilt offering*
> (Leviticus 14:17).

Yeshua (Jesus) is the Lamb of our guilt offering and the blood from his sacrificial death, along with the anointing oil, is not just placed on the lobe of our right ear, on the thumb of our right hand, and on the big toe of our right foot, we are completely washed in his blood and we are clothed and empowered by the Holy Spirit of the Almighty. John the Baptist gave notice of the coming of the life-changing Holy Spirit: —

I baptize you with water for repentance, but he who is coming after me is mightier than I, whose sandals I am not worthy to carry. He will baptize you with the Holy Spirit and fire (Matthew 3:11).

Then Yeshua, (Jesus)—the One of whom John was speaking—said to his first committed followers: —

I am sending upon you the promise of my Father; so stay here in the city until you have been clothed with power from on high (Luke 24:49).

And when they had prayed, the place where they were assembled together was shaken; and they were all filled with the Holy Spirit, and they spoke the word of God with boldness (Acts 4:31).

And so every true believer in Yeshua (Jesus) is transformed from their inherited state of being born a leper to that of being cleansed and anointed as a holy priest to serve God Most High and being part of *"the commonwealth of Israel"* (Ephesians 2:12), which is *"the Israel of God."*

Twelve spies

At this stage Israel has been delivered from bondage to the Egyptian Pharaoh; was led by God Almighty's pillar of fire by night and His pillar of cloud by day as the Israelites traipsed through the wilderness and came into the wilderness of Paran (Numbers 13:3), which is at the southern edge of the Promised Land. The Lord God told Moses to send men to spy out the land of Canaan and report on whether the people are few or many, weak or strong, and whether the cities were open or fortified.

Moses sent twelve man, each man a leader in his tribe, whom Moses instructed to begin their survey in the south and then go up into the hill country. Moses told them to note if the land was fertile, rich or lean, and to make an effort to bring back some of its fruit. The scouts spied out all the land from the wilderness of Zin to Rehob, near the entrance to Hamath before coming to Hebron where the descendants of the Anakim (giants) lived. The scouts came to the Valley of Eshcol (Eshcol means Cluster) and it was the season for the first ripe grapes. The men cut down a shoot of a grape vine with a single cluster of grapes, which they carried on a pole between two men, along with some pomegranates and some figs.

> (The cluster of grapes is traditionally presented as being so huge that it needed to be carried by two men on a pole; this is pure myth. The cluster of grapes, the pomegranates and the figs were carried on a pole between two men in order that the fruit not be crushed while the survey was being completed, before it was presented before Moses and all of Israel.)

The twelve scouts spied out the land of Canaan for forty days before returning to Moses and Aaron and all the Israelite community at Kadesh, in the wilderness of Paran. The scouts said, "We surveyed the land where you sent us and it really does flow with milk and honey, and this is some of its fruit":—

However, the people who live in the land are strong, and the towns are fortified and very large; and moreover, we saw the descendants of Anak there. The Amalekites live in the land of the Negev; the Hittites, the Jebusites, and the Amorites live in the hill country; and the Canaanites live by the sea, and along the Jordan (Numbers 13:28–29).

Caleb, one of the twelve scouts, quieted the people before Moses, and said, *"Let us go up at once and occupy it, for we are well able to overcome it"* (Numbers 13:30). Then the men who had gone up with him said:—

We are not able to go up against this people, for they are stronger than we are. So they brought an unfavorable report of the land that they had spied out, saying, "The land that we have gone through as spies is a land that devours its inhabitants; and all the people that we saw in it are of great size. There we saw the Anakim, the giants who come from the Nephilim, and we seemed like grasshoppers in our own eyes, and so we seemed in their eyes"

(Numbers 13:31–33).

Then all the Israelite community wailed a loud cry, and the people wept that night. All the people of Israel grumbled and complained against Moses and Aaron. The whole community said to them, "If only we had died in the land of Egypt! Or if only we had died in this wilderness! Why is the Lord *bringing us into this land, to fall by the sword? Our wives and our little ones will become spoil. Would it not be better for us to go back to Egypt?" And they said to one another, "Let us choose a leader and go back to Egypt"* (Numbers 14:1–4).

Moses and Aaron fell on their faces before the whole assembly of the children of Israel. Caleb and Joshua, who were among those who had spied out the land, tore their clothes and said to all the congregation of the Israelites: —

The land that we went through as spies is an exceedingly good land. If the Lord *God is pleased with us, He will bring us into this land and give it to us, a land that flows with milk and honey. Only, do not rebel against the* Lord *God Almighty; and do not fear the people of the land, for they are no more than bread for us; their protection is removed from them, and the* Lord *God is with us. Do not fear them." Then the whole congregation threatened to stone them with stones* (Numbers 14:7–10).

Then the glory of the Lord God of Israel appeared to all the Israelites at the doorway of the tent of meeting, and the Lord said to Moses: —

How long will this people despise me? How long will they refuse to believe in me, in spite of all the signs that I have done among them? I will strike them with the plague and disinherit them, and I will make of you a nation greater and mightier than they

(Numbers 14:11–12).

Then Moses pleaded for all the people before the Lord and said, "If you kill all these people in one blow the Egyptians will surely hear of it and tell the inhabitants of the land they heard that you walk among the people and that your pillar of fire and your pillar of cloud goes before them; however they will think that you were unable to bring them into the land promised to them with an oath so you killed them all in the wilderness. Please pardon the iniquity of this people, according to the greatness of your mercy, just as you have forgiven this people, from Egypt until now" (Numbers 14:13–19). Then the Lord God said:—

I do forgive, just as you have asked, nevertheless—as I live, none of the people who have seen My glory and the signs that I did in Egypt and in the wilderness, and yet have tested Me these ten times and have not obeyed My voice, shall see the land that I swore to give to their ancestors. None of those who despised Me shall see it; however, my servant Caleb, because he has a different spirit and has wholly followed Me, I will bring into the land into which he scouted, and his descendants shall possess it. Now, since the Amalekites and the Canaanites live in the valleys, turn tomorrow and set out for the wilderness by the way to the Red Sea (Numbers 14:20–25).

And the Lord God Almighty spoke to Moses and to Aaron, saying:—

How long will this wicked congregation complain against Me? I have heard the kvetching of the Israelites, which they kvetch against Me. Say to them, "As I live," says the Lord, "I will do to you the very things I heard you say: your dead bodies shall fall in this very wilderness; and of all your number, from twenty years old and upward, who have complained against me, not one of you shall come into the land in which I swore to settle you, except Caleb son of

Jephunneh and Joshua son of Nun. But your little ones, who you said would become spoil, I will bring in, and they shall know the land that you have despised. And as for you, your dead bodies shall fall in this wilderness. And your children shall be shepherds in the wilderness for forty years, and shall suffer for your faithlessness, until the last of your dead bodies is buried in this wilderness. According to the number of the days in which you spied out the land, forty days, for every day a year, you shall bear your iniquity, forty years, and you shall know my displeasure." I, the L{ORD} *God of Israel have spoken; surely I will do this to all this wicked congregation gathered together against me: in this wilderness they shall come to an end; and in this wilderness they shall die*
(Numbers 14:26–35).

As for the men whom Moses sent to spy out the land, who returned and made all the congregation of Israel complain against Moses by bringing a bad report about the land—the ten men who brought an unfavorable report about the land—died by a plague before the L{ORD}. Joshua and Caleb alone remained alive of those who were sent to scout out the land (Numbers 14:36–38).

When Moses told all this to the Israelite community, the people mourned greatly. They rose early in the morning, saying, "We are here; we have sinned but we shall now go up to the heights of the hill country, to the land that the L{ORD} God promised to our forefathers." However, Moses said, "Why do you continue to transgress the commands of the L{ORD} God Almighty? You will not succeed for the L{ORD} is not with you. Do not go up; do not let yourselves be struck down by your enemies. The Amalekites and the Canaanites will confront you and you will fall by the sword; because you have turned back from following the LORD God, the LORD God of Israel will not be with you." However, they presumed to go up to the heights of the hill country, even though neither the ark of the covenant of the LORD, nor Moses had left the camp. Then the Amalekites and the Canaanites who lived in that hill country came down, fought and defeated them, pursuing them as far as Hormah (Numbers 14:39–45).

Israel trudged through the wilderness for forty years, following God Almighty's pillar of fire at night and the pillar of cloud by day, by which He made a way before Israel and determining when the congregation should make camp and when it should break camp. From time to time the LORD God Almighty would set Israel down and, through Moses, issue further commandments, statutes, laws and decrees, largely concerning sacrifices and offerings.

In time there came challenges to the leadership of Moses and Aaron, which brought halts to the journeying of the entire community. Even Aaron and his sister Miriam questioned the right of Moses to be the mouthpiece of God Almighty, saying, "Has the LORD God only spoken through Moses? Has he not also spoken through us?" (Numbers 12:2) This upset the LORD because Moses was special, and the LORD called Moses, Aaron and Miriam to the tent of meeting and He cane down to the doorway in a pillar of cloud and God Almighty said to Aaron and Miriam:—

Hear My words: When there are prophets among you, I the LORD make Myself known to them in visions; I speak to them in dreams. Not so with My servant Moses; he is entrusted with all My house. With him I speak face to face—clearly, and not in riddles; and

> he sees the form of the LORD God Almighty. Why then were you not afraid to speak against My servant Moses?" And the anger of the LORD was kindled against them, and He departed (Numbers 12:6–9).

When the cloud lifted from the tent, Miriam had become leprous. When Aaron turned towards Miriam and saw that she was leprous, as white as snow, Aaron said to Moses, "Oh, my LORD, do not punish us for a foolish sin that we have committed. Do not let her be like a baby born dead, whose flesh is half consumed when it comes out of its mother's womb." And so Moses cried out to the LORD, "O LORD God of Israel, please heal her." However, the LORD said to Moses:—

> If her father had spit in her face, would she not bear her shame for seven days? Let her be shut out of the camp for seven days (Numbers 12:14).

So Miriam was shut out of the camp for seven days and Israel did not break camp until the seven days had lapsed and Miriam was brought back into the camp again.

A more serious challenge to the leadership of Moses and Aaron came from Korah, Dathan and Abiram, Levites, who had gathered two hundred and fifty men, all leaders in the congregation of Israel, to oppose the leadership of Moses and Aaron. Korah said to Moses, "You have gone too far. All of the community is holy and the LORD God is among them, so why do you exalt yourselves above the assembly of the LORD?" Moses said to them, God Almighty has allowed you to approach Him, and all the Levites with you; but now you seek the priesthood as well!" Moses then summoned Dathan and Abiram to the tent of meeting, but they said, "We will not come! Is it too little that you have brought us up out of a land flowing with milk and honey to kill us in a wilderness, that you must also lord it over us?"

Moses then said, "Tomorrow we shall see who is allowed to approach the LORD God. Each one take his censer and put fire on it, and incense on the fire, and present it before the LORD God, two hundred and fifty censors and Korah's and Aaron's censors also." Korah assembled the congregation of Israel at the door of the tent of meeting, and the glory of the LORD appeared to the whole congregation. Then God Almighty spoke to Moses and to Aaron, saying: "Separate yourselves from this congregation, so that I may consume them in a moment." But Moses and Aaron fell on their faces and pleaded for the life of the congregation. Then God Almighty spoke to Moses saying: "Tell the congregation: 'Get away from around the homes of Korah, Dathan, and Abiram.'" Then Moses got up and went to Dathan and Abiram; and the elders of Israel followed him. And he said to the congregation of Israel, "Get away from the tents of these evil men, and do not touch anything of theirs, in case you get destroyed because of their sins." So the congregation moved away on every side from the tents of Korah, Dathan, and Abiram, and Dathan and Abiram came out and stood defiantly in the entrances of their tents with their wives, their children, and their little ones. Then Moses said, "This is how you will know that the LORD has sent me to do these works, for I have not done them of my own will. If these men die a natural death, or if they share the fate of all men, then God Almighty has not sent me. However, if He does something new, and the earth opens its mouth and swallows them along with everything they have, and they go down alive to the grave, then you will know that these men have despised the LORD God of Israel!"

As Moses finished speaking, the ground that was under the rebels split open, and the earth opened up and swallowed them, along with their households, and all of Korah's men, and all their goods. The rebels and all that they had went down alive into the abode of the dead, and the earth closed up over them. So the rebels perished from among the congregation and all the Israelites who were around them fled at their cries, saying, "What if the earth swallows us also?" Then a fire went out from the LORD God and consumed the two handed and fifty men who offered incense with their censors (Numbers 16:1–35).

Forty-year death march

The entire adult population of the congregation of Israel, from twenty years old and upward, with the exception of Joshua and Caleb, was prohibited from entering Canaan, the Promised Land, due to their faithlessness. Their lot was to die in the desert wilderness. It is impossible to know the exact number of those who came out of Egypt, therefore we cannot know the exact number of the adult population that was to die in the wilderness. However, using Scripture we do have an accurate starting point for our guesstimations: Excluding the tribe of Levi which was not numbered: —

> *from twenty years old and upward, everyone able to go to war in Israel—their whole number was six hundred three thousand five hundred fifty. The Levites, however, were not numbered by their ancestral tribe along with them"* (Numbers 1:45–47).

Borrowing from what was written earlier: "in most populations, females would make up approximately fifty – fifty-one percent of the population, so we can now safely double the number given for those males able to bear arms, which gives us one million two hundred seven thousand one hundred." To this we must guesstimate a number for those who were either too old or too feeble to bear arms, so let us say forty-five thousand, which brings us to one million two hundred fifty-two thousand one hundred. Now we must guesstimate the number of Levite men and women who were part of the faithless adult population of Israel. Originally, there were twenty-two thousand male Levites one month old and upwards (Numbers 3:39) and using the fifty – fifty-one percent rule for females there would also have been some twenty-two thousand females of the Levite tribe, one month old and upwards, giving a total of forty-four thousand Levites, but how many would have been part of the faithless generation?

Trying to put a believable number on those who perished in the wilderness is difficult. For sure, the six hundred three thousand five hundred and fifty warriors would have perished as would their fifty – fifty-one percent female counterparts. Conservatively, the older adult generation, those above fighting age or too weak to fight, must surely have been around three hundred thousand persons, and perhaps seven thousand male Levites and seven thousand female Levites would have been part of the faithless generation. Thus this writer guesstimates a possible one million five hundred twenty one thousand one hundred (1,521,100) Israelites dying in the wilderness.

Adam Clarke (*Adam Clarke's Commentary, Electronic Database. Copyright (c) 1996 by Biblesoft*), seemingly the only other effort at calculating this event, gives his figure at "over 1,078,000 Israelites (600,000 men, 400,000 wives, 45,000 Levite men, 33,000 Levite wives, plus adults among the mixed multitude died during the wilderness wandering." However, Clarke's figures are hard to reconcile because it was the entire adult population that was faithless, not just the warriors and their wives; and there were only *"twenty-two thousand"* male Levites one month old and upward (Numbers 3:39) when Israel began her wilderness wandering so it is hard for this writer to see how forty-five thousand Levite males and thirty-three thousand Levite wives became part of Clarke's figures.

Nevertheless, those who died in the wilderness definitely exceeded one million souls—likely nearer to one and a half million. However, not all the wilderness casualties died one at a time, Israel's habitual *kvetching* cost many lives. Israel complained that they did not have meat to eat so God Almighty sent an enormous quantity of quail that covered the ground all around the community:—

However, while the meat was still in their mouths, before it was consumed, the anger of the God Almighty was kindled against the people, and He struck the people with a very great plague. So that place was called Kibroth-hattaavah (קברות-התאוה), because there they buried the people who had the craving for meat (Numbers 11:33–34).

From Mount Hor Israel set out for the Red Sea, in order to go around the land of Edom. But the people became impatient and they *kvetched* against God Almighty and against Moses:—

Why have you brought us up out of Egypt to die in the wilderness? For there is no food and no water, and we loathe this worthless manna." Then God Almighty sent fiery serpents among them, and they bit the people, so that many of Israel died
(Numbers 21:4–6).

While Israel was encamped at Shittim, the people went whoring with the daughters of Moab and they ate and bowed down to the gods of Moab; they yoked themselves to Baal of Peor, which infuriated God Almighty and His anger was kindled against Israel. God Almighty said to Moses:—

Take all the chiefs of the people and hang them in the sun before Me, that My fierce anger may turn away from Israel (Numbers 25:4).

Then Moses said to the judges of Israel:—

Each of you kill those of his men who have yoked themselves to Baal of Peor (Numbers 25.5).

One of the people of Israel brought a Midianite woman to his family, in the sight of Moses and in the sight of the whole congregation of Israel weeping at the entrance to the tabernacle (tent) of meeting. When Phinehas, the nephew of Aaron the priest, saw it, he got up, took a spear in his hand and went after them. Phinehas entered the tent where they were having sex and pierced both of them, the Israelite and the Midianite woman, through the belly. Thus the plague on the house of Israel was stopped. Nevertheless, *"those who died by the plague were twenty-four thousand"* (Numbers 25:6–9).

Now, we are left with at least one and a quarter million Israelites who must die a natural death in the wilderness.

A Hebrew year has twelve months; six twenty-nine-day months, and six thirty-day months, making a total of three hundred and fifty-four days, which, if we multiply this by forty we get 14,160—fourteen thousand one hundred and sixty days. So, if we amortize 1.25 million deaths over 14,160 days we arrive at a minimum of 88—eighty-eight deaths per day, sometimes more, sometimes less. However, Hebrew practice is for the immediate family of the deceased to sit shiva for seven days, which is seven days of formal mourning. But grieving does not end with the seven days of sitting shiva, grieving goes on for much longer, but burial of the deceased should be within twenty-four hours of death. However, when we have eighty-eight deaths in one day there will be eighty-eight families mourning and wailing for seven days and burying their dead, and these will be joined by a further eighty-eight families the next day and a further eighty-eight families the day following that, until on the seventh day of shiva for the first family of the deceased there are 616—six hundred and sixteen *families* wailing and weeping for their departed ones. This would continue daily, sometimes more families sitting shiva and burying their dead, sometimes less families sitting shiva and burying their dead—for forty years.

Israel had no one to blame other than themselves, they brought the misery upon their own heads. The ones who stayed true to God Almighty also had to grin and bear it, but God Almighty took care of those who cared for Him. In the Promised Land Caleb could say to Joshua:—

I am today, eighty-five years old. I am still as strong today as I was on the day that Moses sent me to scout the land; my strength now is as my strength was then, for war, and for going and coming

(Joshua 14:10b-11).

Where have all the flowers gone?

At first, the progeny of Jacob (Israel) in Egypt totaled seventy-three persons—including Joseph and his children Manasseh and Ephraim—and, despite the Egyptian genocide carried out against the Israelite boys, the number of Israelites multiplied rapidly, so much so that the Egyptians were afraid of them. Ultimately almost two million Israelites marched out of Egypt to freedom.

Israel's history goes back thousands of years, as does that of China and India. However, the population of China in 2018 was 1.393 *billion* and the population of India in 2018 was 1.353 *billion*, while the *worldwide* Jewish population for the same year was 14.7 *million*. Had the nation of Israel walked in the ways of God Almighty, it could easily have been as populous as China or India today. The reason that it is not is because of its sin and the consequential punitive punishments that God Almighty metered out.

For when your judgments are in the earth, the inhabitants of the world will learn righteousness

(Isaiah 26:9b).

Judgement is part of the redemptive way God Almighty deals with His people and the world. Unless His judgements hit the earth, people do not learn righteousness. Listen to what God Almighty says to Israel through Ezekiel:—

*Prophesy against Israel, say to her this is what the Lord God Almighty says: "I am coming against you,, and I will draw My sword out of its sheath and **will cut off both righteous and wicked**. Because I will cut off from you both righteous and wicked, My sword*

> *will go against all flesh from the south to the north. All flesh shall know that I the LORD God have drawn My sword out of its sheath and it shall not be sheathed again"* (Ezekiel 21:2–5).

We all know about the Holocaust, and the above Scripture could also fit that time of mass murder, which was the worst genocide ever committed in world history, yet even with that and the various pogroms carried out in Eastern Europe it remains impossible to explain the vast difference between the populations of Israel, China and India, which all have similar lengths of history.

From the very beginning God Almighty warned Israel what would happen to them if they did not heed and obey Him. The generation that died in the wilderness is but an example. How many more Hebrews would there be today if that approximately one and a half million Israelites had not died aeons ago through unfaithfulness? It is not just the loss of lives, it is the loss of all their progeny. As a card-carrying Israeli it is not easy for this writer to show the glaring sinfulness of this nation. Like the generation that died in the wilderness, which brought the tragedy upon its own head, it is largely the same for Israel after thousands of years. We turn to the Bible in order to document the gravity of the people's sin, which is ongoing.

However, in order to appreciate God Almighty's promises we must first understand His character: —

> *God is not a mortal that he should lie, or a human being, that he should change his mind. Has He promised, and will He not do it? Has He spoken, and will He not fulfill it?* (Numbers 23:19).

God Almighty is faithful to fulfill His promises. And it matters not whether His promises are for good or for bad,

He is faithful to fulfill them. We know from the divine record that He fulfilled His promises to destroy Israel and the holy city of Jerusalem, and this is also borne out by world history. God Almighty told Israel what blessings would fall to them if they followed after Him and obeyed His voice, and He spelled out what would befall them if they chose not to obey His voice. It was a conditional covenant. The blessings were conditional upon Israel obeying God Almighty, and the curse was conditional upon them disobeying Him. This very important section of Scripture is included here in its entirety—it should be carefully and thoughtfully read by Jew and non-Jew alike, because it is the very foundation upon which Israel is built:—

> *Now it shall come to pass, if you diligently obey the voice of the LORD your God, to observe carefully all His commandments which I command you today, that the LORD your God will set you high above all nations of the earth.*
>
> *And all these blessings shall come upon you and overtake you, because you obey the voice of the LORD your God:*
>
> *1 **Blessed** shall you be in the city, and blessed shall you be in the country.*
>
> *2 **Blessed** shall be the fruit of your body, the produce of your ground and the increase of your herds, the increase of your cattle and the offspring of your flocks.*
>
> *3 **Blessed** shall be your basket and your kneading bowl.*
>
> *4 **Blessed** shall you be when you come in, and blessed shall you be when you go out.*

5 The Lord God will cause your enemies who rise against you to be defeated before your face; they shall come out against you one way and flee before you seven ways.

6 The Lord God will command the blessing on you in your storehouses and in all to which you set your hand, and He will bless you in the land which the Lord your God is giving you.

7 The Lord God will establish you as a holy people to Himself, just as He has sworn to you, if you keep the commandments of the Lord your God and walk in His ways. Then all peoples of the earth shall see that you are called by the name of the Lord God, and they shall be afraid of you. And the Lord God will grant you plenty of goods, in the fruit of your body, in the increase of your livestock, and in the produce of your ground, in the land of which the Lord God Almighty swore to your fathers to give you.

8 The Lord God will open to you His good treasure, the heavens, to give the rain to your land in its season, and to bless all the work of your hand. You shall lend to many nations, but you shall not borrow. And the Lord God will make you the head and not the tail; you shall be above only, and not be beneath, if you heed the commandments of the Lord your God, which I command you today, and are careful to observe them. So you shall not turn aside from any of the words which I command you this day, to the right hand or to the left, to go after other gods to serve them. But it shall come to pass, if you do not obey the voice of the Lord your God, to observe carefully all His commandments and His statutes which I command you today, that all these curses will come upon you and overtake you:

1 **Cursed** *will you be in the city, and cursed shall you be in the country.*

2 **Cursed** *will be your basket and your kneading bowl.*

3 **Cursed** *will be the fruit of your body and the produce of your land, the increase of your cattle and the offspring of your flocks.*

4 **Cursed** *will you be when you come in, and cursed will you be when you go out. The LORD God will send on you cursing, confusion, and rebuke in all that you set your hand to do, until you are destroyed and until you perish quickly, because of the wickedness of your doings in which you have forsaken Me. The LORD God will make the plague cling to you until He has consumed you from the land which you are going to possess.*

5 *The LORD God will strike you with tuberculosis, with fever, with inflammation, with severe burning fever, with the sword, with scorching, and with mildew; they will pursue you until you perish. And your heavens which are over your head will be bronze, and the earth which is under you will be iron.*

6 *The LORD God will change the rain of your land to powder and dust; from the heaven it will come down on you until you are destroyed.*

7 *The LORD God will cause you to be defeated before your enemies; you will go out one way against them and flee seven ways before them; and you will become troublesome to all the kingdoms of the earth.*

8 *Your carcasses will be food for all the birds of the air and the beasts of the earth, and no one will frighten them away.*

9 *The* Lord *God will strike you with the boils of Egypt, with tumors, with the scab, and with the itch, from which you cannot be healed.*

10 *The* Lord *God will strike you with madness and blindness and confusion of heart. And you will grope at noonday, as a blind man gropes in darkness; you will not prosper in your ways; you will be only oppressed and plundered continually, and no one will save you.*

11 *You will betroth a wife, but another man will lie with her; you will build a house, but you will not dwell in it; you will plant a vineyard, but will not gather its grapes.*

12 *Your ox will be slaughtered before your eyes, but you will not eat of it; your donkey will be violently taken away from before you, and will not be restored to you; your sheep will be given to your enemies, and you will have no one to rescue them.*

13 *Your sons and your daughters will be given to another people, and your eyes shall look and fail with longing for them all day long; and there will be no strength in your hand.*

14 *A nation whom you have not known will eat the fruit of your land and the produce of your labor, and you will be only oppressed and crushed continually. So you will be driven mad because of the sight which your eyes see.*

15 *The* Lord *God will strike you in the knees and on the legs with severe boils which cannot be healed, and from the sole of your foot to the top of your head.*

16 *The* L<small>ORD</small> *God will bring you and the king whom you set over you to a nation which neither you nor your fathers have known, and there you will serve other gods—wood and stone. And you will become an astonishment, a proverb, and a byword among all nations where the* L<small>ORD</small> *God will drive you.*

17 *You will carry much seed out to the field and gather but little in, for the locust will consume it.*

18 *You will plant vineyards and tend them, but you will neither drink of the wine nor gather the grapes; for the worms will eat them.*

19 *You will have olive trees throughout all your territory, but you will not anoint yourself with the oil; for your olives will drop off.*

20 *You will beget sons and daughters, but they will not be yours; for they will go into captivity.*

21 *Locusts will consume all your trees and the produce of your land.*

22 *The alien who is among you will rise higher and higher above you, and you will come down lower and lower. He will lend to you, but you will not lend to him; he will be the head, and you will be the tail. Moreover all these curses will come upon you and pursue and overtake you, until you are destroyed, because you did not obey the voice of the* L<small>ORD</small> *your God, to keep His commandments and His statutes which He commanded you. And they will be upon you for a sign and a wonder, and on your descendants forever. Because you did not serve the* L<small>ORD</small> *your God with joy and gladness of heart, for the abundance of everything, therefore you will serve your enemies,*

*whom the L*ORD *God will send against you, in hunger, in thirst, in nakedness, and in need of everything; and He will put a yoke of iron on your neck until He has destroyed you.*

*23 The L*ORD *God will bring a nation against you from afar, from the end of the earth, as swift as the eagle flies, a nation whose language you will not understand, a nation of fierce countenance, which does not respect the elderly nor show favor to the young.*

*24 And they will eat the increase of your livestock and the produce of your land, until you are destroyed; they will not leave you grain or new wine or oil, or the increase of your cattle or the offspring of your flocks, until they have destroyed you. They will besiege you at all your gates until your high and fortified walls, in which you trust, come down throughout all your land; and they will besiege you at all your gates throughout all your land which the L*ORD *your God has given you.*

*25 You will eat the fruit of your own body, the flesh of your sons and your daughters whom the L*ORD *your God has given you, in the siege and desperate straits in which your enemy will distress you.*

26 The sensitive and very refined man among you will be hostile toward his brother, toward the wife of his bosom, and toward the rest of his children whom he leaves behind, so that he will not give any of them the flesh of his children whom he will eat, because he has nothing left in the siege and desperate straits in which your enemy will distress you at all your gates.

27 The tender and delicate woman among you, who would not venture to set the sole of her foot on the ground because of her delicateness and sensitivity, will refuse to the husband of her bosom, and to her son and her daughter, her placenta which comes out from between her legs and her children whom she bears; for she will eat them secretly for lack of everything in the siege and desperate straits in which your enemy will distress you at all your gates.

28 *If you do not carefully observe all the words of this law that are written in this book, that you may fear this glorious and awesome name, The LORD Your God, then the LORD God will bring upon you and your descendants extraordinary plagues—great and prolonged plagues—and serious and prolonged sicknesses. Moreover He will bring back on you all the diseases of Egypt, of which you were afraid, and they shall cling to you. Also every sickness and every plague, which is not written in the book of this law, will the LORD God bring upon you until you are destroyed.*

29 **You will be left few in number, whereas you were as the stars of heaven in multitude**, *because you would not obey the voice of the LORD your God. And it shall be, that just as the LORD God rejoiced over you to do you good and multiply you, so the LORD God will rejoice over you to destroy you and bring you to nothing; and you will be plucked from off the land which you go to possess.*

30 *Then the LORD your God will scatter you among all peoples, from one end of the earth to the other, and there you will serve other gods, which neither you nor your fathers have known— wood and stone. And among those nations you will find no rest, nor*

> *will the sole of your foot have a resting place; but there the* LORD *God will give you a trembling heart, failing eyes, and anguish of soul.*
>
> *31 Your life shall hang in doubt before you; you shall fear day and night, and have no assurance of life. In the morning you will say, "Oh, that it were evening!" And at evening you will say, "Oh, that it were morning!" because of the fear which terrifies your heart, and because of the sight which your eyes see.*
>
> *32 And the* LORD *God will take you back to Egypt in ships, by the way of which I said to you, "You will never see it again." And there you will be offered for sale to your enemies as male and female slaves, but no one will buy you* (Deuteronomy 28:1–68).

After making the blessings and curses known to Israel, God Almighty also said:—

> *I call heaven and earth as witnesses today against you, that I have set before you life and death, blessing and cursing; therefore choose life, that both you and your descendants may live; that you may love the* LORD *your God, that you may obey His voice, and that you may cling to Him, for He is your life and the length of your days; and that you may dwell in the land which the* LORD *God swore to your fathers, to Abraham, Isaac, and Jacob, to give them*
>   (Deuteronomy 30:19–20).

Everything that God Almighty listed among the blessings and the curses came upon Israel, the nation was blessed when it walked according to God Almighty's laws and commandments, and the nation was cursed when its leaders turned their backs upon Israel's Maker and Sustainer of its life. Much of Israel's history reads like a horror story as king after king thumbed his nose at the Giver of life.

Cause and Effect

(Much of the content in this next section has also appeared in a chapter entitled *The Indictment of Israel* in *The Wall: Prophecy, Politics and Middle East "Peace"*: Bennett Ramon, Shekinah 2000.)

Israelis, together with most Jews living in the *galut* (exile) would dearly love to see Israel return to the golden days of David and Solomon. Under David Israel rose to the peak of its military power. Under Solomon Israel rode the crest of splendor's wave and no other nation or king could approach being its equal. However, with the passing of the years following Solomon's death, Israel's military might disappeared. Its majestic glory was trampled in the dust under the feet of a seemingly unending line of conquering armies. Solomon's magnificent gold-encrusted temple in Jerusalem was sacked and burnt, and the inhabitants throughout the length and breadth of the Land died either from the sword, famine and disease, or were taken away by their conquerors into captivity. Israel became a reproach and a byword to all the nations round about. And this happened not just once, but two times.

Seventy years following the first devastation and exile of Israel, God Almighty, as His word foretold, brought His "good figs" (Jeremiah 24:4–7) people back to the Land. Israeli life began anew and, in time, another great temple was built, whose latter glory was said to surpass Solomon's (Haggai 2:9). However, with the passing of time, the same pattern of events took place, and Jerusalem, with its second magnificent temple, was completely destroyed. Millions more Israelis died from the sword, famine and disease, or were taken away to another land by their conquerors.

This writer is an Israeli citizen living in Jerusalem for more than four decades. Throughout that length of time he has had to suffer listening to many Jews berating Gentiles (non-Jews) for every calamity that has ever befallen the Jewish people. The sufferings of the Jewish nation throughout its history is, according to many Jews, almost entirely attributable to the non-Jew Gentiles. Rabbis, however, do teach that the second destruction of Jerusalem was due to the Jews not treating their brethren in accordance with the law of Moses. Apart from this one confession of Jewish shortcomings toward each other—which is far from the real reason for Jerusalem's destruction—the Jews apparently feel their conduct throughout the ages has been rather blameless.

An ultra-Orthodox rabbi from New York had the *chutzpah* (nerve) to seriously tell this writer a story about the two types of animals in the Bible, the clean and the unclean (Leviticus 11:1–8). He began by paraphrasing the biblical passages and said animals that chew the cud and have cloven hooves are clean animals. He said those chewing the cud but not having cloven hooves or those having a cloven hoof but not chewing the cud are unclean animals. He then said:—

> We Jews are the clean animals, we are righteous inside and out, but Gentiles are related to the pig that wallows in its own filth.

No doubt a good number of Israelis, along with other Jews in the *galut*, would readily concur with the rabbi.

Jewish law prohibits Jews being buried alongside non-Jews, and if any non-Jew is inadvertently buried in a Jewish cemetery very effort is to be made to move the corpse to a non-Jewish plot; and Israel's Chief Rabbi ruled in 2021 that if this was not possible, a fence should be erected between the non-Jew's burial place and that of Jews interred at the same place.

Jewish loathing of non-Jews is seemingly put aside in the Jewish quest to gain converts from among the non-Jew Gentiles, which has been ongoing for more than two thousand years. Some Jewish organizations believe that without further adherents (converts) to Judaism the Jewish religion will eventually die out.

Arnold Eisen, chancellor of the Jewish Theological Seminary, wrote a *Wall Street Journal* Op-Ed for July 24, 2014 titled "Wanted: Converts to Judaism." In the article, Eisen wrote: —

> I am asking the rabbis of the Conservative movement to use every means to explicitly and strongly advocate for conversion, bringing potential converts close and actively making the case for them to commit to Judaism. I am asking Jewish leaders to provide the funding needed for programs, courses and initiatives that will place conversion at the center of Jewish consciousness and the community's agenda.

Some Jews obviously believe that if Jews do not spread their religion, Judaism will not survive and therefore will gladly accept those whom they have insulted and vigorously blamed for their troubled history into the Jewish fold. However, the layers of arrogance and pride are peeled away by the biblical records, and many Jews show themselves to be blatant hypocrites. God Almighty Himself responds to those who blame the non-Jews for the tragedies that have befallen the Jewish people: —

> *Why do you complain about your injuries, that your pain is incurable?* ***I have done all this to you because***

your wickedness is so great and your sins are so numerous (Jeremiah 30:15).

Time and time again throughout the biblical narrative the LORD God Almighty shows His vexation and anger at Israel's habitual sinning and apostasy. A very large number of Old Testament pages, even several entire books, are given over to His people's sin and iniquity, together with the description of horrific punishments that were inflicted upon Israel and Judah because of it. God Almighty repeatedly says, *"I beat My fists together in fury"*; and that He either comes, or will come, against them in *"burning anger"*; in *"fury"*; in *"wrath"* to turn them from their wicked ways so that He may *"forgive their iniquity and their sin."* Forgiveness is conditional; repentance must precede forgiveness. Israel was an adulterous nation long before they rejected God Almighty from ruling over them as their King. However, *"the LORD is a God of recompense, He will repay in full"* (Jeremiah 51:56).

Listen to the Divine's indictment of Israel: —

> *the children of Israel **did evil** in the sight of the LORD, and ... the anger of the LORD God was hot against Israel. So He delivered them into the hands of plunderers who despoiled them; and He sold them into the hands of their enemies all around, so that they could no longer stand before their enemies* (Judges 2:11, 14).

> *the children of Israel **did evil** in the sight of the LORD. ...Therefore the anger of the LORD God was hot against Israel, and He sold them into the hand of Cushan-Rishathaim king of Mesopotamia* (Judges 3:7, 8).

> *the children of Israel again **did evil** in the sight of the LORD God. So the LORD strengthened Eglon king of*

*Moab against Israel, because they had **done evil** in the sight of the* L<small>ORD</small>. *Then he gathered to himself the people of Ammon and Amalek and went and defeated Israel* (Judges 3:12, 13).

*the children of Israel again **did evil** in the sight of the* L<small>ORD</small> *God. So the* L<small>ORD</small> *sold them into the hand of Jabin king of Canaan* (Judges 4:1, 2).

*the children of Israel **did evil** in the sight of the* L<small>ORD</small>. *So the* L<small>ORD</small> *delivered them into the hand of Midian ...and the hand of Midian prevailed against Israel* (Judges 6:1, 2).

*the children of Israel again **did evil** in the sight of the* L<small>ORD</small> *God, and ...they forsook the* L<small>ORD</small> *and did not serve Him. So the anger of the* L<small>ORD</small> *God was hot against Israel; and He sold them into the hands of the Philistines and into the hands of the people of Ammon* (Judges 10:6, 7).

*Again the children of Israel **did evil** in the sight of the* L<small>ORD</small> *God, and the* L<small>ORD</small> *delivered them into the hand of the Philistines* (Judges 13:1).

At this point we arrive at where Israel rejects the L<small>ORD</small> God Almighty as its King and demands an earthly king. Saul is chosen, crowned, and later rejected by the L<small>ORD</small> God for rebellion against His commands. Then David enters into history and provides God Almighty with one of the very rare periods where He is obeyed, loved, worshiped and appreciated for Who He is. Of a consequence David is exalted, Israel is delivered from all its enemies, all its territory is restored, and Israel becomes the great power of the region.

Solomon, David's son by Bathsheba, succeeded his father David and began his reign by following in David's footsteps and walking with God Almighty. However, Solomon's lust for women became stronger than his love for God Almighty. In time, Solomon completely cast God aside:—

> *Solomon **did evil** in the sight of the* LORD *God, and ...built a high place for Chemosh the abomination of Moab, on the hill that is east of Jerusalem, and for Molech the abomination of the people of Ammon. And he did likewise for all his foreign wives*
> (1Kings 11:6, 7, 8).

Solomon's sins greatly angered God Almighty, and He determined to tear the kingdom from Solomon, but purposed to leave him Judah because of the promise He had made to David:—

> *And it shall be, when your days are fulfilled, when you must go to be with your fathers, that I will set up your seed after you, who will be of your sons.... He shall build Me a house ... and I will not take My mercy away from him, as I took it from him who was before you* (1Chronicles 17:11, 12, 13).

Solomon's lust for women turned his heart away from the One who had exalted him, and his sowing of rot and apostasy into Israel's soul was to bring forth a bumper crop. The nation, however, was to pay a most terrible price for Solomon's sins. Upon Solomon's death, his son Rehoboam became king over all Israel, but God Almighty's resolve to rip ten of the tribes away and give them to Jeroboam, Solomon's former servant (1Kings 11:26) was inflexible. God Almighty sent Ahijah the prophet to Jeroboam:—

> *Behold, I will tear the kingdom out of the hand of Solomon and will give ten tribes to you (but he shall have one tribe for the sake of My servant David, and*

for the sake of Jerusalem, the city which I have chosen out of all the tribes of Israel), because they have forsaken Me, and worshiped Ashtoreth the goddess of the Sidonians, Chemosh the god of the Moabites, and Milcom the god of the people of Ammon, and have not walked in My ways to do what is right in My eyes and keep My statutes and My judgments
(1Kings 11:31–33).

Rehoboam was subsequently left only with Judah to rule. Even so, he still chose to walk the same evil path as his father Solomon had done. Disaster was about to begin stalking the Land:—

*Rehoboam the son of Solomon reigned in Judah. ...Now Judah **did evil** in the sight of God Almighty, and they provoked Him to jealousy with their sins which they committed, more than all that their fathers had done. For they also **built for themselves high places, sacred pillars**, and **wooden images on every high hill and under every green tree**. And there were also perverted persons* (male and female shrine prostitutes, sodomites) *in the land. They did according to all the abominations of the nations which the* LORD *God had cast out before the children of Israel. It happened in the fifth year of King Rehoboam that Shishak king of Egypt came up against Jerusalem. And he took away the treasures of the house of the* LORD *and the treasures of the king's house; he took away everything*
(1Kings 14:21–26).

Jeroboam reigned over ten of the twelve tribes of Israel, but his sins were greater than all those who had preceded him. He provoked God Almighty to such extreme anger that the LORD God sent Ahijah the prophet to him saying:—

> *Thus says the LORD God of Israel: I exalted you from among the people, and made you ruler over My people Israel, and tore the kingdom away from the house of David, and gave it to you ... but **you have done more evil than all who were before you**, for you have gone and **made for yourself other gods and molded images to provoke Me** to anger, and have cast Me behind your back—therefore behold! I will bring disaster on the house of Jeroboam, and will cut off from Jeroboam every male in Israel, bond and free; I will take away the remnant of the house of Jeroboam, as one takes away refuse until it is all gone. The dogs shall eat whoever belongs to Jeroboam and dies in the city, and the birds of the air shall eat whoever dies in the field; for the LORD God has spoken!*
> (1Kings 14:7, 8, 9–11).

Only five kings—Asa (2Chronicles 14:2), Jehoshaphat (2Chronicles 17:1, 6), Jotham (2Chronicles 27:1-2), Hezekiah (2Chronicles 29:1–2) and Josiah (2Chronicles 34:1-2), all from Judah—followed *the Holy One of Israel* during their reigns. Hezekiah succeeded to the throne of Judah following the death of his father Ahaz:—

> *who did not do what was right in the eyes of the LORD, as his father David had done, but he walked in the ways of the kings of Israel. He even made metal images for the Baals, and he made offerings in the Valley of the Son of Hinnom and burned his sons as an offering, and he sacrificed and made offerings on the high places and on the hills and under every green tree…they did not bring him into the tombs of the kings of Israel* (2Chronicles 28:1–27).

Hezekiah had his servants reconsecrate the house of God Almighty following the abominations and desecrations of previous kings:—

> *They began to consecrate on the first day of the first month, and on the eighth day of the month they came to the vestibule of the LORD God. Then for eight days they consecrated the house of the LORD God, and on the sixteenth day of the first month they finished. Then they went in to Hezekiah the king and said, "We have cleansed all the house of the LORD God, the altar of burnt offering and all its utensils, and the table for the showbread and all its utensils. All the utensils that King Ahaz discarded in his reign when he was faithless, we have made ready and consecrated, and behold, they are before the altar of the LORD God."*
>
> *Then Hezekiah the king rose early and gathered the officials of the city and went up to the house of the LORD God* (2Chronicles 29:17–20).

Therefore the house of God Almighty was rededicated and sanctified on the 17th day of the first month—resurrection day, the day mentioned earlier which became a pattern for holy events that honored the LORD.

Every other king followed the evil inclinations of their own hearts and prepared the way for the sky to fall in on Israel. Consider the records:—

*Nadab ...became king over Israel ...and **he did evil** in the sight of the LORD God* (1Kings 15:25, 26).

*Baasha ...became king over all Israel ...**he did evil** in the sight of the LORD God* (1Kings 15:33, 34).

*Ahab ...became king over Israel; and ...**did evil** in the sight of the LORD God, **more than all who were before him*** (1Kings 16:29, 30).

*Ahaziah ...became king over Israel and ...**he did evil** in the sight of the LORD God* (1Kings 22:51, 52).

Jehoram *the son of Ahab became king over Israel at Samaria ...and* **he did evil** *in the sight of the* LORD *God* (2Kings 3:1, 2).

Jehoram *the son of Jehoshaphat began to reign as king of Judah. And he walked in the way of the kings of Israel ...and* **he did evil** *in the sight of the* LORD *God* (2Kings 8:16, 18).

Ahaziah *...became king, and ...**did evil** in the sight of the* LORD *God* (2Kings 8:26, 27).

Jehu *...anointed king ...over Israel. But Jehu* **took no heed to walk in the law** *of the* LORD *God of Israel* (2Kings 9:2, 3, 10:31).

Jehoahaz *...became king over Israel ...and* **he did evil** *in the sight of the* LORD *God* (2Kings 13:1, 2).

Jehoash *...became king over Israel ...and* **he did evil** *in the sight of the* LORD *God* (2Kings 13:10, 11).

Jeroboam *...became king ...and* **he did evil** *in the sight of the* LORD *God* (2Kings 14:23, 24).

Zechariah *...reigned over Israel ...and* **he did evil** *in the sight of the* LORD *God* (2Kings 15:8, 9).

Menahem *...became king over Israel, and ...**he did evil** in the sight of the* LORD *God* (2Kings 15: 17, 18).

Pekahiah *...became king over Israel ...and* **he did evil** *in the sight of the* LORD *God* (2Kings 15:23, 24).

Pekah *...became king over Israel ...and* **he did evil** *in the sight of the* LORD *God* (2Kings 15:27, 28).

Hoshea *...became king of Israel ...and* **he did evil** *in the sight of the* LORD *God* (2Kings 17:1, 2).

Manasseh *...became king, and ...**he did evil** in the sight of the* LORD *God, according to the abominations of the nations* (2Kings 21:1, 2).

Amon ...became king, and ...he did evil in the sight of the LORD God (2Kings 21:19, 20).

Jehoahaz ...became king, and ...he did evil in the sight of the LORD God (2Kings 23:31, 32).

Jehoiakim ...became king, and he ...did evil in the sight of the LORD God (2Kings 23:36, 37).

Jehoiachin ...became king, and he ...did evil in the sight of the LORD God (2Kings 24:8, 9).

Zedekiah ...became king, and he ...also did evil in the sight of the LORD God (2Kings 24:18, 19).

What a terrible indictment of the kings of Israel and Judah! The people were to learn the truth of the proverb: —

Righteousness exalts a nation, but sin is a reproach to any people (Proverbs 14:34).

When Israel walked before God Almighty in righteousness, it was exalted as a nation. When it stiffened its neck and stubbornly insisted on walking in its own ways and the ways of the nations, it suffered the consequences. For Israel and Judah the fruit of sin became increasingly costly and bitter to the taste. All of the doom and gloom in this book is necessary for the reader to understand why there are so few Jews in the world today. God Almighty said He would destroy them and their cities and remove them from the land if they did not walk in His ways and obey His commands. And so He did.

Valley of Tears

Israelis, together with other Jews living outside the Land, bemoan the sufferings of the Jewish people. Yet, few there are who would have the honesty to say: "We brought it upon ourselves by the many sins we committed against God Almighty, the God of Israel—provoking Him to great anger." As we saw earlier, concerning the sin of the Amorites, God Almighty's judgements are not necessarily immediate, God Almighty is patient and does not act rashly, but He will always act, sooner or later.

Israel's recorded history is one of being selected as God Almighty's chosen people—His very own *special treasure*. However, their fear of Him was brief, their backsliding was rapid, and their apostasy was complete. God Almighty sent His prophets to them time and time again to warn them:—

> *And the LORD God of their fathers sent warnings to them by His messengers, rising up early and sending them, because He had compassion on His people and on His dwelling place. But they mocked the messengers of God Almighty, despised His words, and scoffed at His prophets, until the wrath of the LORD God arose against His people, till there was no remedy* (2Chronicles 36:15–16).

> *And the LORD God has sent to you all His servants the prophets, rising early and sending them, but you have not listened nor inclined your ear to hear. They said, "Repent now everyone of his evil way and his evil doings, and dwell in the land that the LORD God has given to you and your fathers forever and ever. Do not go after other gods to serve them and worship*

them, and do not provoke Me to anger with the works of your hands; and I will not harm you. Yet you have not listened to Me," says the LORD God, "that you might provoke Me to anger with the works of your hands to your own hurt" (Jeremiah 25:4–7).

The messages of repentance, however, held not the slightest interest for them: —

they did not obey nor incline their ear, but made their neck stiff, that they might not hear nor receive instruction (Jeremiah 27:23).

Ultimately, the sky fell in on Israel and Judah: —

Therefore He brought against them the king of the Chaldeans, who killed their young men with the sword in the house of their sanctuary, and had no compassion on young man or virgin, on the aged or the weak; He gave them all into his hand
(2Chronicles 36:17).

the anger of the LORD God was aroused against Israel, and He delivered them into the hand of Hazkiael king of Syria, and into the hand of Ben-Hadad the son of Hazael (2 Kings 13:3).

*Thus says the LORD God of Israel: "I have anointed [Jehu] king over the people of the LORD, over Israel." But Jehu took no heed to walk in the law of the LORD God of Israel... In those days **the** LORD God **began to cut off parts of Israel*** (2Kings 9:2, 3, 10:31, 32).

the king of Assyria ...carried Israel away ...the children of Israel had sinned against the LORD their God ...and had walked in the statutes of the nations
(2Kings 17:6, 7, 8).

*For because of the anger of the LORD God this happened in Jerusalem and Judah, till **He finally cast them out from His presence*** (Jeremiah 52:3).

they would not hear, but stiffened their necks, like the necks of their fathers, who did not believe in the LORD *their God. And they rejected His statutes and His covenant ...and went after the nations ...and* **sold themselves to do evil** *in the sight of the* LORD *God, to provoke Him to anger. Therefore the* LORD *God was very angry with Israel, and removed them from His sight; there was none left but the tribe of Judah alone. Also Judah did not keep the commandments of the* LORD *their God, but walked in the statutes of Israel... And the* LORD *God rejected all the descendants of Israel, afflicted them, and delivered them into the hand of plunderers, until He had cast them from His sight. For ...the children of Israel walked in all the sins ...until the* LORD *God removed Israel out of His sight, as He had said by all His servants the prophets. So Israel was carried away from their own land...*
  (2Kings 17:14, 15, 16, 17, 18, 19, 20, 21, 22, 23).

If God Almighty's chosen people would but read His indictment of them, perhaps some might cease to lay the blame for the Jewish nation's woes at the feet of the non-Jewish Gentiles. Many, however, would still concur with the ultra-Orthodox rabbi who said: "We Jews are the clean animals, we are righteous inside and out, but Gentiles are related to the pig that wallows in its own filth." Jesus was handed over to the Romans for crucifixion by such rabbis—partly due no doubt to His scathing indictment of them:—

Woe to you scribes and Pharisees, hypocrites! For you are like whitewashed tombs which indeed appear beautiful outwardly, but inside are full of dead men's bones and all uncleanness (Matthew 23:27).

It was successive centuries of committing sin and doing evil that brought God's punitive judgment upon the whole nation of Israel. A long line of evil, unrepentant kings sank the people deeper and deeper into sin's mire. It is a sad but true fact that a nation will become what its leaders are. Sheep grow fat from feeding on pasture that shepherds lead them into and leave them to graze upon.

It is another sad fact that among the haredi Jews of today, who claim to tremble before God Almighty, a large number of ultra-Orthodox Jews wear the label of a criminal; many are no less corrupt than those who shun the LORD God, especially when it comes to being sexual predators or takers of bribes.

One former ultra-Orthodox Chief Rabbi was imprisoned for financial corruption and a haredi government minister was also imprisoned for financial corruption. This particular former minister served his prison term and the statuary seven years necessary before a re-entering of politics, but is under indictment again today for financial corruption while holding the same ministerial position he had before his imprisonment. These high-ranking shepherds are those who lead the people to graze upon polluted pasture.

More than half of the haredi community is utterly selfish. They refuse to serve in the Israel Defense Forces (IDF) and also reject an alternative community service. Most of the men will not join the Israeli workforce and therefore do not share the tax burden of the Israelis. They practice "reverse birth control" by having sex with their wives when the women are at the peak of their fertility cycle. Consequently, the haredi birthrate is three times that of the average Israeli woman and they receive government financial payments for each child, which rises with each additional child; some families live entirely off child benefits. Haredim often quote the biblical injunction *"Be fruitful and multiply"* given at God's creation of Man (Genesis 1:28), and to Noah after the flood (Genesis 8:17), but that was many, many hundreds of years prior to the giving of the Law and is today used as a mere pretext in order to prise funds out of the government without having to work (other than making the babies). All the child benefits paid are on the backs of the Israelis who work and pay taxes. Most haredi men study *Torah* full time and for this they receive government stipends; the schools being funded by taxpayer money and which do not teach basic education like English, Math, Science, etc., so the men are completely unfit to compete in our commercial, consumer-driven world.

Dozens of ultra-Orthodox men, primarily rabbis, have been indicted for multiple sexual offenses against both women and men, and, in a departure from the norm, a woman who is a member of the Gur Hassidic sect, was recently extradited from Israel to Australia to face seventy-four counts of child sexual abuse of girls at an ultra-Orthodox school where she had been the director. An ultra-Orthodox member of Israel's parliament, the leader of an ultra-Orthodox political party, has been indicted by the Police for interfering with the proceedings in attempts to prevent the woman's extradition. The outwardly projected righteousness of the ultra-Orthodox Jewish community is largely a sham righteousness as God Almighty pointed out through Ezekiel: *"for with their mouth they show much love, but their hearts pursue their own gain"* (Ezekiel 33:31b). Yeshua (Jesus) was not fooled by the haredim of the day; he said to the people: —

For I tell you, unless your righteousness exceeds that of the scribes and Pharisees, you will never enter the kingdom of heaven (Matthew 5:20).

Some can perhaps feel the pain of God's heart more acutely than others, but from the following scripture everyone should get some idea of just how provoked God Almighty has been by Israel and Judah:—

*And the LORD God spoke by His servants the prophets, saying, "Because Manasseh king of Judah has done these abominations (he has acted more wickedly than all who were before him, and has also made Judah sin with his idols), therefore thus says the LORD God of Israel: Behold, I am bringing such calamity upon Jerusalem and Judah, that whoever hears of it, both his ears will tingle. And I will stretch over Jerusalem the measuring line of Samaria and the plummet of the house of Ahab; I will wipe Jerusalem as one wipes a dish, wiping it and turning it upside down. So **I will forsake the remnant of My inheritance and deliver them into the hand of their enemies**; and they shall become victims of plunder to all their enemies, **because they have done evil** in My sight, and have provoked Me to anger since the day their fathers came out of Egypt, even to this day"*

(2Kings 21:10–15).

As a parent, the LORD laments over His stubborn children:—

Hear, O heavens, and listen, O earth; for God Almighty has spoken: I reared children and brought them up, and they have rebelled against Me. The ox knows its owner, and the donkey its master's food trough; but Israel does not know, My people do not understand (Isaiah 1:2–3).

(The children that God Almighty reared had their childhood in Egypt, their youth in the desert, and adulthood from Joshua to Samuel.)

It was mentioned earlier that there were only five kings who followed the ways of God Almighty with a whole heart. One of those kings, Josiah, endeavored with all of his might to bring the people of Judah back to a vibrant relationship with their Maker. Despite Josiah's wholehearted love and obedience, however, *the Holy One of Israel* would not relent of the punitive destruction He had purposed to bring because of the sins of former kings:—

Now before him there was no king like [Josiah], who turned to the LORD *God with all his heart, with all his soul, and with all his might, according to all the Law of Moses; nor after him did any arise like him. Nevertheless the* LORD *God did not turn from the fierceness of His great wrath, with which His anger was aroused against Judah, because of all the provocations with which Manasseh had provoked Him. And the* LORD *God said, "I will also remove Judah from My sight, as I have removed Israel, and will cast off this city Jerusalem which I have chosen, and the house of which I said, 'My name shall be there'"* (2Kings 23:25–27).

And God Almighty fulfilled His promise of doom down to the last letter. His warnings of impending judgment were clearly and persistently delivered by His prophets, but all those warnings were ignored. The joyful, unrepentant years of sin finally reaped a bountiful harvest of destruction, death, pain and misery:—

You have fed them with the bread of tears, and given them tears to drink in great measure (Psalms 80:5).

One hundred and fourteen years later the same drama was to be acted out again, with the same tragic and terrible consequences, this time it was Judah's turn. The unrepentant people of the Land only had themselves to blame for what befell them:—

Righteousness exalts a nation, but sin is a reproach to any people (Proverbs 14:34).

It is worth noting that the conquerors of Israel and Judah were considered "servants" of God Almighty carrying out His decrees of punishment against His disloyal people:—

*Thus says **the great king, the king of Assyria**: "Have I now come up without the LORD against this place to destroy it?" The LORD said to me, 'Go up against this land, and destroy it'* (2Kings 18:25).

*Thus says the LORD, "I will take all the tribes of the north, and **Nebuchadnezzar the king of Babylon, My servant**, and I will bring them against this land, against its inhabitants, and against the nations all around, and will utterly destroy them, and make them an object of horror and of hissing, and an everlasting disgrace"* (Jeremiah 25:9).

Israel is like scattered sheep; The lions have driven him away. First the king of Assyria devoured him; Now at last this Nebuchadnezzar king of Babylon has broken his bones.

Therefore thus says the LORD of armies, the God of Israel: "Behold, I will punish the king of Babylon and his land, as I have punished the king of Assyria" (Jeremiah 50:17–18).

*How **the hammer of the whole earth** is cut down and broken! How Babylon has become an object of horror among the nations!* (Jeremiah 50:23).

The powerful kings of Assyria and Babylon were Servants of God Almighty who actually *"**worked for Me**"* (Ezekiel 29:20), but God Almighty crushed them both because they *"touched the pupil* of His eye" (Zechariah 2:8).

Today, after seventy-three years of statehood, Israel's Jewish population, stands at less than seven million and the current total for all worldwide Jewry is less than fifteen million. The reason Israel is not as populous as China and India, both of which have similar lengths of history, is because of her sin and the inevitable punitive punishments that God Almighty handed out to her because of it.

The Apostle Paul, a Pharisee, in Romans 9:29, quoting the Prophet Isaiah, extols the graciousness of God in leaving to Israel even a small remnant of its people:—

Unless the L*ord* *of hosts (armies) had **left to us a very small remnant**, we would have become like Sodom, we would have been made like Gomorrah*

(Isaiah 1:9).

Israel in antiquity was so wicked, so corrupt, that only the few God-fearing people left in it prevented the name and nation from being swept into extinction like Sodom and Gomorrah. The vast shortfall between Israel's current population and that of India's or China's is entirely due to Jewish stiff-necked rebellion against walking in the ways of *the Holy One of Israel*. It should also be borne in mind that it is no new thing for God Almighty to abandon the greater part of the Jewish nation, when corrupt, and confine his blessing and favor to the righteous, God-fearing few.

Yeshua (Jesus) the *King of the Jews* is not only rejected today, but even the knowledge of Him has been scrubbed from Israeli minds. The nation has gone a whoring after a golden calf of materialism, and much prefer to have godless secular humanists rule over them. God is good, *God is love*, but He will not suffer being trifled with indefinitely by modern Israel.

Despite God Almighty promising Israel that His blessings will *"come upon you and overtake you,"* they stubbornly chose not to obey Him, thereby choosing death. God's patience ran out: —

> *I earnestly exhorted your fathers in the day I brought them up out of the land of Egypt, until this day, rising early and exhorting, saying, "Obey My voice." Yet they did not obey or incline their ear, but everyone followed the dictates of his evil heart; therefore I will bring upon them all the words of the covenant, which I commanded them to do, but which they have not done* (Jeremiah 11:7–8).

Both Israel and Judah were conquered and destroyed, one hundred and twenty years apart. The survivors of the first conquest were taken into captivity in Assyria, and later the survivors of the conquest of Judah were taken to Babylon. Remember, George Santayana said: "Those who do not learn from history are doomed to repeat it." Israel did not learn and, therefore, repeated it.

Another repeat performance of refusing God's ways brought another destruction to a reestablished Israel in the first century C.E., and Israel went back into exile among the nations for almost 1,900 years. However, true to His word God Almighty brought Israel back again into His land once more and established them for a third time. But how long will it be before His patience wears thin with Israel again?

Following the establishment of the modern state of Israel in 1948, the Israelites today are largely turning their backs on God Almighty again. A large percentage of Israelis today have no belief in God Almighty at all, and they are openly antagonistic to anything that smells like religion. Many could not care less for His land either; they just want to be left alone to do their own thing—*"As it is written, 'The people sat down to eat and drink, and rose up to play'"* (1Corinthians 10:7).

There is, of course, a remnant in Israel today who follow *the Holy One of Israel* with a whole heart, just as there was a remnant who wholeheartedly followed Him in days of yore. However, that God-fearing remnant in yesteryear did not prevent the destructions and horrors that came upon the nation. Neither will today's God-fearing remnant prevent another horrific catastrophe if God Almighty's patience really gets tested.

Israel and the nations seriously and urgently need to consider the fact that God Almighty has not changed with the passing of the years: *"I am the LORD, I do not change"* (Malachi 3:6). What does need to change is the heart of the nation of Israel, the heart of every Jew in every part of the world. The behavioral patterns that provoked *the Holy One of Israel* to anger yesterday will also provoke Him to anger today. The terrible consequences that followed yesterday's events will, over time, repeat themselves again due to similar events taking place today. What has been written here should be taken very, very seriously.

Home at last

The establishment of the modern state of Israel in 1948 clearly shows that God Almighty is true to His word and has not, nor will He ever, cast off His people due to their grievous sin. That which was foretold by the prophets came to pass:—

> *Who has ever heard of such a thing? Who has ever seen such a thing? Can a country be brought forth in one day? Can a nation be born in a single moment? Yet as soon as Zion was in labor she brought forth her children. Shall I open the womb and not deliver? says the LORD God; shall I, the one who delivers, shut the womb? says your God* (Isaiah 66:8–9).

"Can a country be brought forth in one day?"

(Isaiah 66:8).

Indeed it could. In 1914, during the Great War, British forces faced a shell crisis through a lack of cordite, an essential ingredient of high explosive. British guns were reduced to firing only four shells per day and it seemed as if the war could be lost. Chaim Weizemann, a noted Jewish chemist—a lecturer at Manchester University and considered to be the father of industrial fermentation—was summoned to the British War Office by Winston Churchill, the First Lord of the Admiralty, and asked to produce thirty thousand tons of cordite.

By May of 1915 Weizemann showed that he could convert a hundred tons of grain into twelve tons of acetone, which meant that he needed two hundred and fifty thousand tons of grain in order to fulfill Churchill's request. Big breweries were subsequently commandeered by the government for their fermentation abilities and, along with the existing factories, two new factories were built. With every available government facility at his disposal, Weizmann manufactured a synthetic cordite that actually produced a higher explosive than cordite from acetone.

Together, all the factories working on the project produced more than ninety thousand gallons of acetone a year, enough to feed the war's ravenous demand for cordite.

From 1914 to 1918, Churchill's Royal Navy and the British Army fired two hundred and forty-eight million shells. After Weizemann had produced the requested amount of cordite he was asked what he wanted as compensation. His reply was:—

> If Britain wins the battle for Palestine, I ask for a national home for my people in their ancient land.

Britain, which had been saved from pending disaster by Weizmann, agreed to his request. Shortly afterward, on November 2, 1917, the British Foreign Minister Arthur James Balfour, on behalf of the government, issued a statement that had been approved by the Cabinet:—

> His Majesty's Government view with favour the establishment in Palestine of a national home for the Jewish people, and will use their best endeavors to facilitate the achievement of this object, it being clearly understood that nothing shall be done which may prejudice the civil and religious rights of existing non-Jewish communities in Palestine or the rights and political status enjoyed by Jews in any other country.

When the great war was over the Ottoman Empire was broken up and Britain received the Mandate to govern Palestine.

Home at last 237

The League of Nations (forerunner of the United Nations) narrowly voted to partition what was then known as Palestine between Jews and Arabs.

> (The Roman Empire conquered and occupied Israel in 63 B.C.E and after a failed, drawn-out uprising against Rome that ended in 135 C.E., Jews were banished from Jerusalem and the city was renamed Ælia *Capitolina* after the Emperor Hadrian, whose name was *Ælius*. The whole land was renamed *Syria Palæstina*, which made a bogus Syrian and Philistine connection to the land. *Palæstina* is Latin for Philistia, the territory of the Philistines, which, in time, became Anglicized to Palestine. Thousands of Jews remained in Palestine and over time they were joined by other Jews who came in a steady trickle to drain the swamps and start agriculture. Palestinian Arabs sold Jews their least favorable, unwanted pieces of scrub land and marshes at exorbitant prices. The Jews transformed the land and Arabs came from near and far to work for what they considered to be the high wages paid by the enterprising Jews.)

The League of Nations met on November 29, 1947 and a majority of member states voted to partition Palestine, which was in fact the real starting point of today's ongoing Israel-Palestinian conflict.

Even though the Jews had been promised the entirety of Palestine, seventy-seven percent had been cut off and proclaimed to be Trans-Jordan (now Jordan), the remaining twenty-three percent was to be divided between the Jews and the Arabs with the larger part going to the

Arabs, but the Arabs and the Arab League rejected the overture outright. The Jews were still willing to settle for a minuscule, truncated state, believing that gaining only a small piece of Palestine was infinitely better than having no piece of Palestine, and therefore no homeland. However, the country of Jacob's progeny was born in less than a day; it took only the hours necessary for the vote to take place.

"Can a nation be born in a single moment?" (Isaiah 66:8).

Yes indeed. It took less time than the vote which brought forth the country. On May 14, 1948, David Ben-Gurion, the first prime minister of the modern state of Israel, formerly declared to its citizens, and to Jews everywhere, that the longed-for state of Israel was now actual. On hearing the news, Jews from all over the world began moving to their new homeland. Eight hundred and sixty thousand of hose living in Arab lands were forced out, leaving with only what they could carry in their hands and on their backs, they were dispossessed of their valuable properties and possessions by the Arab rulers.

> *Shall I bring to the point of birth and not cause delivery. Shall I who cause delivery shut up the womb? says your God* (Isaiah 66:9).

On the day following the announcement of the establishment of the state of Israel, on May 15, 1948 seven mechanized Arab armies—equipped and trained by Britain and some led by British officers—attacked the nascent state of Israel in a bid to destroy it (British tanks tried to block the advance of Israel's fighters during their attack on Jaffa and RAF fighter planes, flying out of Egypt, engaged the fledgling Israeli air force over Israeli positions in the Sinai. But God Almighty, *"the holy One of Israel,"* was with His people and they miraculously endured the onslaught. It was Israel's War of Independence.

Home at last

There were only a relative few fighting men in Israel at the outbreak of the war and even fewer weapons; not a single tank or artillery piece was to be seen apart from the Davidka, a highly inaccurate, tremendously noisy mortar which, when fired, the Arab forces thought it to be an atom bomb. Israel's airforce consisted of four obsolete fighter-bombers of which two were shot down the first day.

What weapons Israel did have were almost all homemade and not enough of those for each fighter to have his or her own personal weapon. Israel improvised, using whatever was available. Over the weeks and months thousands of men and women arrived from overseas and joined Israel's war effort. Aircraft, tanks, and weapons were bought, purloined, or made from discarded scrap.

The war continued until July 1949 and the Israel Defense Forces (IDF) became established and a small airforce was born. Over a period of months armistice (truce) agreements were signed with Egypt, Jordan, Syria and Lebanon. Other protagonists just withdrew their forces, handed over their sectors to allies, and went home. Jordan had won the battle for Jerusalem, denying Jews access to the Western Wall and the Temple Mount for the first time in over a thousand years. The Jordanians dynamited forty-eight synagogues (the great Hurva synagogue being one of them) and used Jewish gravestones as latrines. After an armistice was signed between the two sides, Jerusalem remained divided under Israeli and Jordanian rule.

However, despite the loss of Israel's burgeoning agriculture to a war that destroyed its choicest fields, orchards and vineyards, it was still a huge win for the struggling state. Israel had pushed the invading armies (apart from Jordan) back well beyond the partition lines, increasing its territorial size by almost three hundred percent, and that against overwhelming odds that were better equipped and very highly trained.

The Arabs looked upon the armistice lines as mere lines from which they would launch their real war of extermination. The War of Independence did nothing to stop terror strikes across Israel's borders, which came from three fronts: (Egyptian, Lebanese and Syrian), which has ultimately become a way of life for Israelis.

The next Arab-Israel war was the 1956 Suez crisis, when Egyptian President Gamal Abdel Nasser nationalized the British-French controlled Suez Canal, because he needed the funds generating from the Canal's use in order to build the Aswan Dam, which the West had refused to finance due to Nasser's embrace of the Soviet Union and its support for rebels in the French colony of Algeria. Israel was put in the frontlines of the war when Britain and France persuaded it to use its troops to liberate the Canal in a tripartite invasion of Egypt. Israel was to capture the Canal after which British and French paratroopers would be dropped behind them to secure it. Israeli troops invaded the Sinai Peninsular on November 29, easily defeating the Egyptian forces in Sinai. Two days later Britain and France began bombing Egyptian positions and British and French paratroopers and marines took up strategic positions in the Canal zone.

The United Nations quickly passed a resolution calling for a ceasefire and both the United States and the Soviet Union demanded, along with threats of sanctions and a possible Soviet nuclear intervention, for British, French and Israeli troops to withdraw. Israel received nothing from its venture and Britain and France were replaced by the United States and Soviet Union as powerbrokers in the Middle East.

In 1967, Arab nations began massing their troops and war machinery on Israel's borders, encircling it in preparation for another attempt at liquidating the Jewish presence in the region. The leader of the Palestine Liberation Organization (PLO) told *Time* magazine that he did not expect there to be any survivors among the Jews.

Greatly outnumbered in men and equipment, the Israeli security cabinet decided to initiate a pre-emptive strike to ensure Israel's survival. On June 5, Israel launched the now famous pre-emptive strike against the Arab airforces; in a matter of hours Israel destroyed several hundred of the enemies' warplanes in four countries that were standing invitingly in the open on the tarmac at the Arab airfields. The surprise attack completely crippled the Arabs' ability to wage war from the air. Israeli forces then engaged and routed the Arab forces of five nations in just six days, totally liquidating the Arab war machine, much to the chagrin of the Soviet Union that had manufactured and sold the weapons and machinery. It was a lightening-fast war that stunned the world and greatly increased the expanded territorial holdings that had followed the War of Independence, again by over three hundred percent. It was a war that changed the balance of power in the Middle East, and one that has thus far brought Israel a fifty-four-year-long headache.

Israel endeavored to trade most of its captured land, wishing to exchange it for peace with the Arab nations. Defense Minister Moshe Dayan famously said that he was "waiting for a telephone call from the Arab world," but Israel's peace overture was turned down in no uncertain fashion. An official statement from the Arab League summit held from August 29 to September 1, 1967 in Khartoum, Sudan, from a unified leadership of thirteen Arab states, said quite distinctly: *"No peace with Israel; No negotiations with Israel; No recognition of Israel."* This became known as "The 3 No's of Khartoum." Dayan gave up waiting for the expected telephone call and was laid to rest in October 1981.

After the devastation Israel unleashed upon their armies in June 1967 the Arab leadership began planning for yet another war for the liquidation of Israel, but this time they decided to use a little more cunning and follow the Israeli opening of the Six Day War. This latest war was to be a surprise attack by multiple armies on Yom Kippur (The Day of Atonement), the holiest day of the year for Jews.

The Soviet Union had rearmed the Arab armies with more sophisticated weaponry and therefore it had a stake in the outcome of the war. On October 6, 1973 a coalition of Arab armies launched a surprise invasion of Israel when Israelis were fasting and attending synagogues; and there was no way of communicating the danger to the nation.

On Yom Kippur all radio and television stations are shut down and there are no newspapers, and virtually no one would answer a telephone even if it should it ring. The IDF command could only go door-to-door to inform its troops; it took three days for Israel to mobilize its forces.

Egyptian forces with hundreds of tanks poured across the Suez Canal and wreaked havoc against the sparse few of Israeli troops left on duty in the Sinai Peninsular on that most solemn day. Syrian forces, also with hundreds of tanks swept across the Golan and engaged the Israeli defenses there. Seven smaller Arab armies had joined the fray, coming across the Jordan. Hundreds of Israeli troops died before the nation even knew it was at war.

Israel drove the invaders back, with the fiercest fighting being in northern Israel, the Sinai Peninsular and on the Golan (both of which Israel had captured in the Six-Day War; and which now created buffer zones for Israeli cities against the invading hordes). By day ten of the war the IDF had forced the invaders back across the borders of Israel; by day nineteen it was pressing on toward Cairo, having encircled Egypt's ninth army and the city of Suez; Israel was also shelling the outskirts of Damascus.

The Soviet Union contacted American President Richard Nixon at the White House and told him that if he did not stop the Israeli forces it would itself intervene with nuclear weapons. Not willing to risk a nuclear confrontation with the Soviet Union Nixon tried coaxing, then threatened Israel into stopping its forces, thus ending the war on October 25. However, Israel was then occupying a good deal of land on the Egyptian side of the Suez and was occupying a sizable portion of Syria's Bashan above the Golan, so at the end of the war Israel's territory had increased by some two thousand one hundred square kilometers (eight hundred and eighty-one square miles).

Without doubt, Israel's consistent military defeats of coalitions of Arab armies—all of which have been overwhelmingly greater in troop numbers, machines, and weapons—is clear evidence of God Almighty's hand being upon Israel, like it was in the Israelite conquest of Canaan under Joshua:—

Moses My servant is dead. Now proceed, go over this Jordan, you and all this people, into the land that I am giving to them, to the people of Israel forever
(Joshua 1:2).

In November 1977 Anwar Sadat, the president of Egypt who had overseen the Yom Kippur War against Israel, became the first Arab leader to officially visit Israel. Sadat spoke to the Israeli Knesset (Parliament) saying "No more war" and began negotiations with Israel's prime minister Menachem Begin for a peace settlement. A Peace Agreement was signed in March 1979 and Egypt became the first Arab nation to make peace with Israel, both Sadat and Begin were awarded the Nobel Peace Prize for their efforts. Unfortunately, Egypt's peace with Israel was and is highly unpopular throughout the Arab world and Egypt was suspended from the Arab League for ten years, from 1979 to 1989. The peace treaty with Israel was largely the reason of Anwar Sadat's assassination on October 6, 1981. Sadat was assassinated by Egyptian soldiers during a victory parade held each year in Cairo to celebrate Egypt's crossing of the Suez Canal at the launch of the Yom Kippur War.

On October 26, 1994 Israel and Jordan also signed a Peace Agreement, but both the Egyptian peace and the Jordanian peace have over time been somewhat icy, with rare bilateral meetings between leaders and officials. Egyptian parliamentarians have said that Israel is Egypt's only enemy, and Jordanian parliamentarians regularly call for Jordan's peace treaty with Israel to be cancelled.

In September 2020 came bombshell news that United Arab Emirates (UAE) had signed a peace agreement, known as the Abraham Accords, between Israel, and the United Arab Emirates. President Donald Trump had been involved with the deal, which was crafted by Jared Kushner, Trump's son-in-law. The Abraham Accords—so named because Israel and Arab nations have common ancestry in Abraham—is a treaty of peace with full normalization of ties between the moderate UAE and Israel. Since the signing of the Abraham Accords a number of projects between the parties have been commissioned and activated and the outlook for the future of the relationship is the brightest and most promising of the three peace treaties. More goodwill has been shown to Israel by the UAE in the few months since the signing than has ever been shown toward Israel by Egypt or Jordan. The UAE obtained dozens of America's latest Stealth Fighter Bombers and other top weapons due to its signing of the peace agreement with Israel.

Under the umbrella of the September 2020 Abraham Accords was also a Normalization of Relations agreement with the Kingdom of Bahrain: a Declaration of Peace, Cooperation, Constructive Diplomatic and Friendly Relations with Israel. Concerns about Iran's growing influence in the region persuaded Bahrain to end its trade boycott of Israel and align itself more toward Israel, becoming the fourth Arab state to recognize Israel. All of the nations that signed peace agreements with Israel under the Abraham Accords are being threatened by Iran for having alied themselves with the "soon to be eliminated illegal zionist entity".

Sudan—the home of the famous "3 No's of Khartoum"—finally capitulated on its hatred of Israel and signed an Abraham Accords' Declaration that "Seeks to end radicalization and conflict to provide all children with a better future." For its part Sudan received millions of dollars from the US to help relieve its massive debt to the World Bank and was taken off the US list of state sponsors of terrorism, a designation that has blocked Sudan's access to international loans. Of late, Sudan says it is not receiving enough money from America; if true this could collapse Sudan's normalization deal with Israel.

Morocco made a deal with President Trump whereby the Kingdom received sovereignty of the entire Western Sahara territory. In exchange the Kingdom agreed to authorize direct flights between Morocco and Israel by Moroccan and Israeli airlines and to allow overflights of each countries airspace. It was also agreed to "Immediately resume full official contacts between Israeli and Moroccan counterparts and establish full diplomatic, peaceful and friendly relations."

President Trump was the prime mover and shaker in the Abraham Accords and it remains to be seen if there will be any follow-ups now that Trump is no longer the star on the world's stage.

Morocco and Israel had long been enjoying quiet relations together and the Abraham Accords could cement these relations further. However, with President Trump awarding sovereignty over the entire Western Sahara to Morocco, which has largely occupied the region since the Spanish withdrew from its protectorate in 1975, apart from the twenty-two percent that the self-proclaimed Sahrawi Arab Democratic Republic (SADR) occupies. The Sahrawi Arab Democratic Republic is represented at the United Nations by the Polisario Front that began an insurgency in 1973 from Mauritania against Spanish control in the region of Western Sahara. Mauritania made peace with the Polisario Front, then Morocco unilaterally annexed Mauritania's portion of Western Sahara. Awarding sovereignty over the whole of the disputed territory in the Western Sahara to Morocco began a new phase in the war for SADR independence in the Western Sahara, which SADR fights for as a homeland. The awarding of sovereignty to Morocco as a reward for peace with Israel has greatly disturbed an Arab hornets nest and many people are going to get stung.

It should be noted that all Arab signatory states to "peace" with Israel through the Abraham Accords had little input into the Arab-Israeli conflict so we can expect little to change there; however, all four Arab states continue as before in their voting pattern of going against Israel at the United Nations.

According to a clear footprint of the six peace treaties signed thus far, peace between Israel and the Arab and Islamic worlds is a delusion. All have signed only for what they could get out of it, not from any heartfelt desire to make an enduring peace with their Jewish neighbor. Of the two leaders who did desire peace—Anwar Sadat and King Hussein of Jordan—Sadat was assassinated for that belief and Hussein's son Abdullah struggles to prevent his ministers from overthrowing him and canceling the treaty.

The toxic anti-Jew, anti-Israel violence manifested throughout the entire world through large and small demonstrations, was gleefully reported upon by the leftist antisemitic news media, by both its print and digital arms. The hate-filled fury broke out during Israel's eleven-day war against Iran's Hamas and Palestinian Islamic Jihad terror proxies in May 2021, which launched well over four thousand missiles at Israel's civilian population centers from Palestinian population centers in Gaza. This clearly constituted a double war crime, but the world by and large stood with the terrorists and condemned Israel for exercising its right to defend itself by airstrikes against Hamas and Islamic Jihad infrastructure in the Gaza Strip.

The LORD God of Israel intended Jacob's progeny to dwell alone as a nation, Israel is the LORD God's own inheritance and was born to be separate from all other nations:—

From the top of the rocks I see him and from the hills I behold him; There! A people dwelling alone, Not reckoning itself among the nations (Numbers 23:9).

Successive Israeli prime ministers, beginning with Yitzhak Rabin in 1993, have made it clear that under their watch Israel should be like all other nations, but *the Holy One of Israel*, the *God of Jacob* will never let it be so. No matter how many peace agreements Israel's liberal leaders sign, Israel will always be alone—alone with her Creator:—

"God Most High, Possessor of heaven and earth"
(Genesis 14:19).

One like the Son of Man

The entire premise of Israel's existence is built upon its adherence to God Almighty's covenant which He made with Israel when He brought His people out of Egypt. Prior to the destruction of Jerusalem Jeremiah reminded Israel of that: —

> *Thus says the L*ORD *God of Israel:* "**Cursed is the man who does not obey the words of this covenant which I commanded your fathers in the day I brought them out of the land of Egypt**, *from the iron furnace, saying, 'Obey My voice, and do according to all that I command you; so shall you be My people, and I will be your God'"* (Jeremiah 11:3–4).

Countless millions died through Israel's disobedience and eventually the people were sent into captivity. The northern kingdom of Israel never returned from captivity, only the survivors from the southern kingdom of Judah, and those from the northern kingdom who came into Judah to follow their God returned; these were the "good figs" of Jeremiah 24:4–7. According to Ezra 2:64–65 and Nehemiah 7:66–67, the number of exiles that returned after seventy years of punitive captivity was forty-two thousand three hundred and sixty (42,360), plus seven thousand three hundred and thirty-seven (7,337) male and female slaves, making a total of forty-nine thousand six hundred and ninety seven (49,697). The "bad figs" of Jeremiah 24:8–10 were destroyed by "the sword, famine and pestilence." The return of the "good figs" took place between 539 B.C.E. and 458 B.C.E., but what goes around comes around and 63 B.C.E Israel was conquered and occupied by Rome because it spurned the ways of its Creator and King.

(It is generally taught that there are "ten lost tribes" of Israel, but this is really not true. It is true that those taken captive to Assyria from the northern kingdom of Israel did not return; however, we see from Scripture that thousands came over to the southern kingdom of Judah from the northern kingdom:—

> *The Levites had left their common lands and their holdings and had come to Judah and Jerusalem, because Jeroboam and his sons had prevented them from serving as priests of the* LORD (2Chronicles 11:14),
>
> *Then he gathered all Judah and Benjamin, and those who dwelt with them from Ephraim, Manasseh, and Simeon, for* **they came over to him in great numbers from Israel** *when they saw that the* LORD *his God was with him* (2Chronicles 12:9).
>
> *They offered at the dedication of this new house of God one hundred bulls, two hundred rams, four hundred lambs, and as* **a sin offering for all Israel**, *twelve male goats, according to the number of the tribes of Israel* (Ezra 6:17).

This is a clear indication that there many from all twelve tribes returned from the Babylonian captivity, because they were counted as being part of Judah; and God

Almighty now sees those that returned as constituting the nation of Israel.)

When God Almighty's *"appointed time had come, He sent forth His Son, born of a woman, born under the law"* (Galatians 4:4). The portrayal of Yeshua (Jesus) is most clearly set forth in the books of Daniel (in Aramaic), in Micah, and his suffering in Isaiah 53, the forbidden chapter, which space does not allow for inclusion here. First Daniel:—

I was watching in the night visions, and One like the Son of Man was coming with the clouds of heaven, and he came to the Ancient of Days and was presented before Him. And to him was given dominion and glory and a kingdom, that all peoples, nations, and languages should serve him; his dominion is an everlasting dominion, which shall not pass away, and his kingdom one that shall not be destroyed

(Daniel 7:13–14).

(In a traditional Jewish commentary on the book of Daniel published by Mesorah Publications, Brooklyn, New York, containing commentary and comments from Talmudic, Midrashic and Rabbinic sources, it has the following to say on the above passage:

"On the clouds of heaven suggests the coming of the Messiah will be a sudden and swift arrival."

The One like the Son of Man is, according to the renowned Rabbi Rashi, "the King Messiah." And Rabbi Yehoshua ben Levi says the "clouds of heaven implies a swift arrival of the Messianic King and if the people do not merit it, it is written elsewhere (Zechariah 9:9) that he will surely come as a poor man and riding upon an ass."

The favorite term Yeshua (Jesus) used to refer to himself was "Son of Man," but rather than using the common Hebrew term for a son of man—*ben adam* (אדם בן) he would most certainly have used the Aramaic—*bar enosh* (בר אנש), which would have shown his divine empowerment and those who heard him use the phrase would immediately reference Daniel 7:13 in their minds and realize the divine import of the phrase. That Yeshua (Jesus) used the Aramaic words for Son of Man (בר אנש) and not the *ben adam* (בן אדם) of Judean Hebrew (יהודית) can be understood by his very usage of those words:—

> *But that you may know that the Son of Man* (בר אנש) **has power on earth to forgive sins**"— *he said to the paralytic, "Arise, take up your bed, and go to your house"* (Matthew 9:6).
>
> *The Son of Man* (בר אנש) **will send out his angels**, *and they will gather out of his kingdom all things that offend, and those who practice lawlessness*
> (Matthew 13:41),

Those listening to Yeshua (Jesus) on those occasions would have known that no mere earthling could forgive sins; and that no mere earthling could send out his angels to root out anarchy from his kingdom.)

Micah foretells the birth of God Almighty's Son, Yeshua (Jesus), in Bethlehem: —

> *But you, Bethlehem Ephrathah, though you are little among the clans of Judah, yet from out of you will come forth to Me the One who is to be ruler in Israel, whose coming forth is from of old, from ancient days, and this One shall be our peace* (Micah 5:2, 4, 5a).

And so in 4 B.C.E. Yeshua (Jesus), God's sacrificial lamb was born. Yeshua (Jesus) was born *into* this world, not *from* it. He was the Word, *"and the Word was with God, and the Word was God. He was in the beginning with God"* (John 1:1), and *"the Word became flesh and dwelt among us"* (John 1:14). And Yeshua (Jesus) began his three-year-plus ministry in 26 C.E. in which he preached the kingdom of God, and made many enemies among the religious leaders. Until Yeshua (Jesus), salvation for the Jews was only possible through strict observance of the Law of Moses. Yeshua (Jesus) ran counter to the religious thought of the day and there were several attempts to stone him and he said to them: —

> *Has not Moses given you the law? Yet none of you keeps the law. Why do you seek to kill me?"*
>
> (John 7:19).

Charging the religious with not keeping the law was tantamount to saying they were cursed, because in the law it is written: —

> *Cursed is the one who does not keep all the words of this law* (Deuteronomy 27:26).

> *For as many as are of the works of the law are under the curse; for it is written, "Cursed is everyone who does not continue in **all** things that are written in the book of the law, to do them"* (Galatians 3:10).
>
> *Yeshua (Jesus) the Messiah (Christ), the Anointed One, has redeemed us from the curse of the law, having become a curse for us, for it is written, "Cursed is everyone who hangs on a tree"* (Galatians 3:13).

Jews claimed that God was their father, but Yeshua (Jesus) contradicted them: —

> *Yeshua (Jesus) said to them, "If God were your Father, you would love Me, for I proceeded forth and came from God, I came not of my own accord, but He sent me"* (John 8:42).

Yeshua (Jesus) made it perfectly clear that he had not come to annul the law of Moses: —

> *Do not think that I have come to abolish the law or the prophets. I have not come to abolish these things but to fulfill them* (Matthew 5:17).

He preached the opposite of destroying the Law: —

> *In truth, I say to you, until heaven and earth pass away, not one letter, not one stroke of a letter, will pass from the Law until all is accomplished.*
>
> *Therefore, whoever breaks one of the least of these commandments, and teaches others to do the same, will be called least in the kingdom of heaven; but whoever does them and teaches them will be called great in the kingdom of heaven* (Matthew 5:18–19).

Yeshua (Jesus) clearly taught that the Law was still operative for all those who chose to live under the Law, and that it would be so until the end of time.

Yeshua (Jesus) came to fulfill what the prophets had foretold, but he ran counter to religious thinking when he said openly to the people:—

> *The law and the prophets were **in force until John the Baptist; since then, the good news of the kingdom of God is being proclaimed*** (Luke 16:16).

There was to be a clean break from the Law and a new regimen established; the old covenant had become obsolete. Yeshua (Jesus) described the new regimen as a new beginning; everything would be new, not patched:—

> *No one sews a patch of unshrunk cloth on an old garment, because the patch will pull away from the garment and the tear will become worse. And no one pours new wine into old wineskins; for the skins will burst and the wine will be spilled and the skins destroyed. Instead, put new wine into new wineskins and both wine and skins are preserved*
> (Matthew 9:16–17).

Under the Law there is no escape, those who failed in one part were guilty of breaking the entire Law; under the new covenant mercy prevailed:—

> *I am writing these things to you so that you may not sin. But if anyone does sin, we have an advocate with the Father, Yeshua (Jesus) Christ, the Messiah, the righteous One* (1John 2:1).

> *If we confess our sins, he is faithful and just to forgive us our sins and to cleanse us from all unrighteousness* (1John 1:9).

The apostle Paul, raised as a Pharisee, puts the Law into perspective:—

> *What purpose then does the law serve? It was added because of transgressions, till the Seed (Yeshua-*

> *Jesus) should come to whom the promise was made; and it was appointed through angels by the hand of a mediator* (Galatians 3:16-19).

During the evening of his arrest, knowing what was about to take place, Yeshua (Jesus) said:—

> *Now My soul is troubled, and what shall I say? "Father, save Me from this hour"? But **for this purpose I have come to this hour*** (John 12:27).

Yeshua (Jesus) expressly came to do his Father's will as it is written of him:—

> *Then I said, "Behold, I have come— In the volume of the book it is written of me— To do Your will, O God"* (Hebrews 10:7; Psalms 40:7).

Just as Isaac was Abraham's *"only son"* (Genesis 22:2, 12, 16), and through him the promises came to Israel, and, ultimately, to the world, so Yeshua (Jesus) was God Almighty's *"only begotten Son"* (John 3:16), and in him *"all the promises of God Almighty are Yes and in him Amen"* (2Corinthians 1:20):—

> *For Yeshua (Jesus) suffered for sins once for all, the righteous for the unrighteous, in order to bring you to God. He was put to death in the flesh, but made alive in the spirit, in which also he went and made a proclamation to the spirits in prison, who in former times did not obey, when God waited patiently in the days of Noah, during the building of the ark, in which a few, that is, eight persons, were saved through water. And baptism, which this prefigured, now saves you—not as a removal of dirt from the body, but as an appeal to God for a good conscience, through the resurrection of Yeshua the Messiah—Jesus Christ*
> (1Peter 3:18–21).

Take a moment to ponder the monumental, absolutely incredible, really stupendous salvation that Yeshua (Jesus) wrought for all mankind. It was not just forgiveness of all sins, past, present and future, and eternal life for all living beings who accept him in their hearts as God Almighty's Son, who died, was buried, and rose from the dead on the third day, but he also descended into the nether world after his death and preached salvation and the kingdom of God to the multitudes who had died previously in their sins; no one was left out.

Jews believe they will inherit salvation by keeping the law of Moses but, as both Scripture and Yeshua (Jesus) says, none keep the law, so for them it is a lose, lose situation unless they receive Yeshua (Jesus) by faith:—

We know that a person is not justified—counted as righteous—by works of the law but through faith in Yeshua the Messiah (Jesus Christ), so we have believed in Yeshua the Messiah (Jesus Christ), in order to be justified by faith in Yeshua (Jesus) and not by works of the law, because by works of the law no one will be justified (Galatians 2:16).

As just said, all those who believe they will receive eternal life through the law are in a lose, lose situation, and to them Yeshua (Jesus), the living Son of the living God, says:—

Therefore I tell you, the kingdom of God will be taken away from you and given to a people that produces the fruits of the kingdom. Whoever falls on this stone will be broken to pieces, and it will crush anyone on whom it falls Matthew 21:43)

The Greek word used here for people is *ethnos* (ἔθνος), which means a multitude of individuals of the same nature or genus, often translated as "nation." The multitude of individuals of the same nature is *"the Israel of God"* (Galatians 6:16) who believe Yeshua (Jesus) is the Messiah and who act in accordance with that belief, The *"stone"* mentioned is Yeshua (Jesus):—

> *"A stone of stumbling, and a rock of offense." They stumble because they disobey the word, as they were destined to do* (1Peter 2:8).

Through the prophet Jeremiah God Almighty promised Israel a new covenant:—

> *"I will make a new covenant with the nation of Israel after I plant them back in their land," says the* L<small>ORD</small> *God Almighty. 'I will put My law within them and write it on their hearts and minds. I will be their God and they will be My people'"* (Jeremiah 31:33).

Yeshua (Jesus) is that new covenant and the only way Jews can get the law within them is by receiving Yeshua (Jesus) into their hearts:—

> *He shall see the labor of his soul, and be satisfied. By his knowledge My righteous Servant shall justify many, for he shall bear their iniquities* (Isaiah 53:11).

Who is a Jew?

We saw very early in this book that God Almighty created Man in His image, and that early Man proved to be far from righteous and that within ten generations:—

God Almighty saw that the wickedness of man was great in the earth, and that every intention of the thoughts of his heart was only evil continually
(Genesis 6:5).

So God began again from scratch. He flooded the earth and used righteous Noah to replenish the earth with humans and the full creation that was carried in the Ark of sanctuary:—

By faith Noah, when he was warned about things not yet seen, with reverent regard, constructed an ark for the deliverance of his family. Through faith he condemned the world and became an heir of the righteousness that comes by faith (Hebrews 11:7).

Ten generations after Noah came righteous Abraham, whom God Almighty called *"My friend"* (Isaiah 41:8), and in Abraham God Almighty had found what He was looking for in Man. God Almighty promised that every human being who has faith like that of Abraham would be deemed righteous by God. In due time our Creator gave His *"only begotten Son,"* who was the Seed of Abraham, to be a sacrificial lamb that all who accept him by faith would be accorded the righteousness of Abraham:—

Now to Abraham and his Seed were the promises made. He does not say, "And to seeds," as of many, but as of one, "And to your Seed," who is Messiah
(Galatians 3:16)).

God honors righteous people. Noah was honored (Genesis 7:1), Abraham was honored (Genesis 26:4–5), Phinehas was honored (Numbers 25:11), David was honored (2Kings 19:34), Caleb was honored (Number 14:24) *et al.* All God-fearing people leave a legacy in their lands.

In 30 C.E. Yeshua (Jesus) was crucified, and in 70 C.E. Jerusalem was sacked by the Romans; the second magnificent temple was burnt to the ground; and the people of Israel began to be widely dispersed among the nations. A distinguished historical source (*Eusebius, Ecclesiastical History*) records that more than sixty thousand Jewish believers in Yeshua (Jesus) fled to Arabia and found refuge in and around Pella at the outbreak of hostilities with the Romans. Yeshua (Jesus) warned His disciples in Matthew 24:16 to *"flee to the mountains,"* and history records:—

> The Christians, warned by these predictions, fled from Jerusalem to Pella, and other places beyond the Jordan; so that there is not evidence that a single Christian perished in Jerusalem.

This book is all about Israel and the Jews, but at this point we are faced with a conundrum. The Jews who believe in Yeshua (Jesus) are more Jewish than the Chief Rabbi of Israel, but the haredim (ultra Orthodox Jews) reject them as apostates because they believe in the Messiah who is written about from A to Z in the *Tanach*—the Hebrew Old Testament Scriptures.

In the New Testament (*Brit HaHadashah*) it is written:—

> *But it is not as though the word of God has failed. For not all who are descended from Israel belong to Israel* (Romans 9:6),

Who is a Jew?

So we must ask the question: Who then belongs to Israel? And here we must differentiate between human thought and God Almighty's response that is sealed in heaven:—

> *For **no one is a Jew who is merely one outwardly**, nor is circumcision outward and physical. But a Jew is one inwardly, and circumcision is a matter of the heart, by the Spirit, not by the letter. His praise is not from man but from God* (Romans 2:28–29).

This is not something new; God Almighty admonished the Israelites in the wilderness:—

> *Circumcise therefore the foreskin of your heart, and be no longer stiff-necked* (Deuteronomy 10:16).

And looking ahead to the days of the New Covenant He says:—

> *And the* LORD *your God will circumcise your heart and the heart of your offspring, so that you will love the* LORD *your God with all your heart and with all your soul, that you may live* (Deuteronomy 30:6).

Looking toward that day the LORD God of Israel says:—

> *A new heart I will give you, and a new spirit I will put within you; and I will remove from your body the heart of stone and give you a heart of flesh*
> (Ezekiel 36:26).

What God Almighty is desiring from Israel is righteous hearts like that of Noah; righteous hearts like that of Abraham; and they will not be gained by:—

> *honoring Me with their mouths, while their hearts are far from Me, and their worship of Me are merely commandments of men learned by rote* (Isaiah 29:13).

> *Israel strives for the righteousness that is based on the law, but does not succeed in fulfilling that law. Why*

> *not? Because they do not strive for it on the basis of faith, but as if it were based on works. They stumble over the stumbling stone, as it is written, "See, I am laying in Zion a stone that will make people stumble, a rock of offense that will make them fall, and whoever believes in him will not be put to shame"*
>
> (Romans 9:31–33).

The stumbling stone is of course Yeshua (Jesus), whom the Rabbis and sages have made offensive for the people, and they therefore stumble over him. Paul the Pharisee writes further:—

> *Brothers and sisters, my heart's desire and prayer to God Almighty for the Jews is that they may be saved. I can testify that they have a zeal for God Almighty, but it is not enlightened. For, being ignorant of the righteousness that comes from God Almighty, and seeking to establish their own, they have not submitted to God Almighty's righteousness. For Messiah (Christ) is the end of the law so that there may be righteousness for everyone who believes*
>
> (Romans 10:1–4).

With the entrance of Yeshua (Jesus) in God Almighty's plan of redemption for Man, there is a hope for all people, not just for those of Jacob:—

> *And now the LORD God says, who formed me in the womb to be His Servant, to bring Jacob back to Him, and that Israel might be gathered to Him, for I am honored in the sight of the LORD God Almighty and my God has become my strength—Indeed He says, "It is too light a thing that you should be My Servant to raise up the tribes of Jacob and to restore the survivors of Israel;* **I will give you as a light to the**

nations, that My salvation may reach to the end of the earth" (Isaiah 49:5–6).

Some years ago we entered a period that is traditionally called The End Times, which in reality is the great and terrible Day of the LORD; and not only Israel will be plowed during this time, but the whole earth will face great pain and upheaval:—

Behold, the day of the LORD comes, cruel, with wrath and fierce anger, to make the earth a desolation and to destroy its sinners from it. For the stars of the heavens and their constellations will not give their light; the sun will be dark at its rising, and the moon will not shed its light.

I will punish the world for its evil, and the wicked for their iniquity; I will put an end to the pomp of the arrogant, and lay low the pompous pride of the ruthless.

I will make people more rare than fine gold, and mankind than the gold of Ophir. Therefore I will make the heavens tremble, and the earth will be shaken out of its place, at the wrath of the LORD of armies in the day of his fierce anger (Isaiah 13.9–13).

There would seem to be little difference between the actions of humans in Noah's and Isaiah's time and that of today's supposedly educated and enlightened population; God Almighty's thoughts today must closely follow His thoughts in Noah's and Isaiah's day:—

God Almighty saw that the wickedness of man was great in the earth, and that every intention of the thoughts of his heart was only evil continually

(Genesis 6:5).

> *Now the earth was corrupt in God's sight, and the earth was filled with violence* (Genesis 6:11).

We should be thankful that He made a promise to Himself after the Flood:—

> *The LORD said in his heart, "I will never again curse the ground because of Man, for the intention of Man's heart is evil from his youth. Neither will I ever again strike down every living creature as I have done"*
> (Genesis 8:21).

However, the Mighty One of Jacob must be deeply saddened when He looks down at us on this earth, saddened at its senseless violence, saddened at its gross inhumanity to man, saddened at its endemic corruption and saddened at His chosen people's rejection of His Son. How long will it be before He vents His anger and fury on us again?

It is a given that Israel will again be punished by the LORD God of Israel for its rebellion against His covenant, in particular its desecrating of the Sabbath; and its allowance of public transport to run on the Sabbath; for opening stores, restaurants and cinemas for trade on the Sabbath; proclaiming and advertising Tel Aviv as the gay (homosexual) capital of the world—*"indulging in sexual immorality and pursuing unnatural lust"*; holding pride (homosexual) parades throughout the county, most offensively to God Almighty in His holy city of Jerusalem, which, with the pride parade, openly thumbs its nose at Him who is *"the holy One of Israel."* There are some who weep at the goings on in Israel, but most are happy with the status quo and this will cost them dearly. God Almighty's ax is going to fall, heads will roll and blood will flow; it is only a matter of time.

Israel is surrounded by heavily-armed mortal enemies, predominantly Iranian proxy armies, which desire to wipe Israel from the map. Israel's Maker and King has repeatedly used powerful nations to punish His rebellious people; however, God Almighty chose Jacob as His inheritance and may not allow His beloved to again be swept from the land that He swore on oath with an upraised hand (Ezekiel 47:14) to give to Abraham, Isaac and Jacob and their descendants forever, despite its ongoing sin and iniquity.

The LORD God will not forsake His people, for His great name's sake, because it pleased the LORD God to make them a people for Himself (1Samuel 12:22).

When the LORD God is with Israel in its wars of defense, Israel crushes its enemies. However, it is not widely recognized by either friend or foe, that Israel's God is not only *"the Holy One of Israel,"* but that He actually dwells among the Israelites and fights for them: *"And the nations will know that I am the LORD, the Holy One IN Israel"* (Ezekiel 39:7b). Therefore the Portion of Jacob, the Maker of all things, whose name is the LORD of armies, could well liken Israel the tribe of His inheritance, to Cyrus king of Persia:—

You are My war club, My battle weapon: with you I break nations in pieces; with you I break kingdoms; with you I break the horse and its rider; with you I break the chariot and the charioteer

(Jeremiah 51:20).

Israel will no doubt suffer both military and civilian casualties, together with wide scale destruction of property in the horrendous fireworks that are about to be lit in the Middle East, but woe, woe to those who are on the receiving end of the LORD God Almighty's wrath for having touched *"the pupil of His eye"* (Zechariah 2:8).

The great and terrible Day of the Lord

The great day of judgement for all nations and peoples is vividly portrayed for us in the book of Revelation. John the revelator opens up be telling us that he was "in the Spirit on the Lord's Day" (Revelation 1:10). This was not a Sunday. John was transported by the Spirit to the great and terrible day of the Lord, which is mentioned twenty-six times in twelve books of the Bible, but depicted in all its power throughout Revelation. John has told us that he was in the Spirit on "the great day of God's vengeance" (Isaiah 61:2), and from Peter's second letter we understand that "with the Lord one day is like a thousand years, and a thousand years like one day" (2Peter 3:8). Of a consequence, this "day of vengeance" will be long protracted.

Moving to Chapter 6 of Revelation we have the opening of the seven seals, which are on the scroll that no one except Yeshua (Jesus) could open:—

> *Now I saw when the Lamb opened one of the seals; and I heard one of the four living creatures (Revelation 4:6, 8, 5:6, 8, 14, 6:1, 6, 7:11, 14:3, 15:7, 19:4) saying with a voice like thunder, "Come!" And I looked, and behold, a **white horse**. He who sat on it had a bow; and a crown was given to him, and he went out conquering and to conquer*
> (Revelation 6:1–2).

> *When He opened the second seal, I heard the second living creature saying, "Come!" Another horse, **fiery red**, went out. And it was granted to the one who sat on it to take peace from the earth, and that people should kill one another; and there was given to him a great sword*
> (Revelation 6:3–4).

*When He opened the third seal, I heard the third living creature say, "Come!" So I looked, and behold, a **black horse**, and he who sat on it had a pair of scales in his hand. And I heard a voice in the midst of the four living creatures saying, "A quart of wheat for a denarius, and three quarts of barley for a denarius; and do not harm the oil and the wine"* (Revelation 6:5–6).

*When He opened the fourth seal, I heard the voice of the fourth living creature saying, "Come!" So I looked, and behold, a **pale green** horse. And the name of him who sat on it was Death, and Hades followed with him. And power was given to them over a fourth of the earth, to kill with sword, with hunger, with death, and by the beasts of the earth* (Revelation 6:7–8).

Most English-language translations have rendered the Greek word cloros (χλωρός) as "a pale horse"; an "ashen horse"; even a "colorless horse," but the word cloros means "pale green" (from which we get our word Chlorophyll, which is made of green pigments from herbs and algae) and translators should have known better; only the NRSV and NET versions have it correct. Is it important? In a word, Yes!

The first horse is WHITE and it is granted to its rider the power to go out conquering and to conquer. The second horse is FIERY RED and its rider is granted the power to take peace from the earth, and that people should kill one another; and there was given to him a great sword. The third horse is BLACK and its rider is granted the power to cause great famine, from which people would obviously die. The fourth horse is PALE GREEN and its rider is Death and Hades and it is granted the power over a fourth of the earth, to kill with sword, with hunger, with death. The reader should now take time to look at flags and emblems of Islamic nations and entities.

The four colors obviously have an important and significant meaning for Islam; however, the nations whose flags have these colors cannot agree (at least publicly) regarding their meaning. Declarations range from the colors representing different Muslim caliphates, but there are differing opinions on which caliphate goes with the black, the white, and the green and leaves no caliphate explanation at all for the red. Black was the standard of Muhammad, the founder of Islam, which likely explains the Islamic State's use of a totally black flag.

There does seem to be a consensus that Red symbolizes blood and martyrdom and that Pale Green symbolizes Islam. But seven centuries ago a Muslim poet summed up the colors with: "White are our acts, black our battles, green our fields, and red our swords."

The *White horse* was to go out conquering and to conquer, which brings to mind the Islamic State's self-declared—albeit short-lived—Islamic caliphate of peace in Iraq and Syria, and the Taliban's conquering of Afghanistan.

The *Red horse* was to take peace from the earth and that people should kill one another, and the rider was given *a great sword*. The *great sword* would surely be the sword of Islam and the *Red horse* has indeed taken peace away from much of the world; where Islamics are slaughtering thousands, even other Muslims.

The *Black horse* has caused hundreds, if not thousands, to die of famine as Western and non-Western forces battle Islamic forces in the Middle East and Africa.

The *Pale Green horse*, whose rider is *Death and Hades*, has power over one fourth of the earth, to kill with sword, hunger and death. The Islamic religion today has some one fourth of the world's inhabitants as adherents who now practice Islam. This writer is not saying, *"Thus saith the* LORD," but it behooves us to look at world events with eyes wide open and to pray for enlightenment. The world is falling apart, disintegrating, before our eyes, and has been doing so for years. For the most part, the mainstream liberal media now publishes false or misleading news; it is a waste of time looking there in order to find out what is really happening. Such wide scale brutal murder of Christians is taking place in many countries making Christians the most persecuted people in the world today, but do not expect to find such news in a godless media.

John Calvin, a French theologian, pastor and reformer during the era of the Protestant Reformation left us some food for thought about why things can go badly for us:

> Since the Devil, who seeks to drain human beings of their God-given spirituality, tries to lull them to sleep, God must employ various stratagems to awaken them. This helps to explain the troubles that afflict the elect: God threatens, chastises, and compels them to remember him by making their lives go badly.

In Chapter 8 of Revelation we read of the *"seven angels who are given seven trumpets"*: —

> *The first angel sounded: And hail and fire followed, mingled with blood, and they were thrown to the earth. And a third of the trees were burned up, and all green grass was burned up* (Revelation 8:7).

We only need to think of the disastrous fires that in recent years have ravaged several countries and wreaked havoc in them, or the calamitous droughts that are affecting rivers and lakes and fish, livestock and agriculture. And so it goes with each of the following five angels sounding his trumpet, which unleash different judgements on the earth, many of which are caused through climate change. God Almighty wants to catch people's attention and get them to look to Him in these days of fear and uncertainty, but more often than not their reaction is like what is written in Revelation: —

> *They were scorched by the fierce heat, and they cursed the name of God who had power over these plagues. They did not repent and give Him glory. The fifth angel poured out his bowl.... People gnawed their tongues in anguish and cursed the God of heaven for their pain and sores. They did not repent of their deeds* (Revelation 16:9–10).

After the first bowls are poured out there is a change in pace: —

> *in the days of the sounding of the seventh angel, when he is about to sound, the mystery of God would be finished, as He declared to His servants the prophets*
>
> (Revelation 10:7).

All critically acclaimed English-language translations render the Greek word *hemera* (ἡμέρα) as *days*, plural. But this word can also mean a single day, a period of time, or a lifetime; the point being that inside the *"day of God's vengeance"* we also have extended periods of time, possibly lifetimes, especially with the seventh trumpet sounding. As mentioned earlier, these End Times are going to be protracted; it could take several years, or even decades for each trumpet period to play out and each bowl of "wrath" to be poured out.

> *Then one of the four living creatures gave the seven angels seven golden bowls full of the wrath of God, who lives forever and ever; and the sanctuary was filled with smoke from the glory of God and from his power, and no one could enter the sanctuary until the seven plagues of the seven angels were completed.*
>
> *Then I heard a loud voice from the sanctuary telling the seven angels, "Go and pour out on the earth the seven bowls of the wrath of God Almighty who lives forever and ever"* (Revelation 15:7–8; 16:1).

There are seven bowls of God Almighty's wrath that are to be poured out upon the earth. One such bowl must surely be the Covid-19 pandemic which (at this time of writing) has taken the lives of over five million people and sickened hundreds of millions more, and, despite triple vaccinations, is seemingly unstoppable and aggressively spreading throughout the world.

A host of deadly diseases, once thought to have been eradicated, such as measles, chicken pox, tuberculosis (TB), bubonic plague, leprosy, and several others have resurrected themselves and patients are now being treated in hospitals throughout the Western world.

Many Christians blame the Devil for every calamity, war and sickness that takes place in the world; however, all of the Bible should be read and not just the parts that they underline:—

I am the LORD, and there is no other. I form light and create darkness; I make peace and create calamity; I am the LORD, who does all these things (Isaiah 45:6–7).

Everything is subject to the voice of God Almighty:—

Remember the former things of old; for I am God, and there is no other; I am God, and there is no one like Me, declaring the end from the beginning and from ancient times things not yet done, saying, "My purpose shall stand, and I will fulfill My intention, calling a bird of prey from the east, the man for My purpose from a far country. I have spoken, and I will bring it to pass; I have planned, and I will do it (Isaiah 46:9–12).

God Almighty planned long ago that His people Israel should know His salvation. He has not rejected Jacob, God may have turned His face away from him, turned His back on the Israelites a time or two and cast them aside because of their wickedness and rebellion against Him and His covenant, but the Jews are and always will be His covenant people and "the pupil of His eye" (Zechariah 2:8). God Almighty has often disciplined His people and has even crushed them in fury on occasions, because history has shown that Israelites are born with an inclination to do evil; however, through Jeremiah the prophet God Almighty tells the whole world that Israel and its people are as eternal as day and night:—

> Thus says the LORD God Almighty, who gives the sun for light by day and the fixed order of the moon and the stars for light by night, who stirs up the sea so that its waves roar—the LORD God of armies is His name: "If this fixed order departs from before me, declares the LORD God, then shall the descendants of Israel cease from being a nation before me forever."
>
> This is what the LORD God says: "If the heavens above can be measured, and the foundations of the earth below can be searched out, then I will cast off all the descendants of Israel for all that they have done, declares the LORD"
> (Jeremiah 31:35–37).

There has always been handful or two of Jacob's offspring who have followed the LORD God with whole hearts. Paul the apostle, a Pharisee, says, "Do you not know what the Scripture says of Elijah, how he pleads with the LORD God against Israel?" Elijah said, "LORD, they have killed your prophets, they have broken down your altars; only I am left, and they are trying to end my life." But what is the Almighty's reply? *"I have kept for Myself seven thousand men who have not bowed their knees to Baal."* And so also at the present time there is a remnant that has been chosen by grace. And if it is by grace, it is no longer by works of the Law, otherwise grace would no longer be grace.

We ask then, has Israel stumbled so as to fall? And the answer is, "Never!" However, through Israel's stumbling salvation has come to the non-Jews, in order to make the Israelites jealous. So if Israel's stumbling means riches for the non-Jews, how much more will the Jews' repentance and conversion mean!

In God Almighty's mind there are only two peoples in the world: the Jewish people and the non-Jewish people of the nations. God Almighty's plan since before time began is to blend the two peoples into one people.

Israel is a cultivated olive tree, non-Jews are all wild olive trees. Breaking off some of the branches of the cultivated olive tree and the grafting in of some wild olive branches represent the current partial rejection of Israel and the corresponding reception of the non-Jews. Some of the branches of Israel were broken off, and non-Jews, being wild olive shoots, are being grafted into Israel and they share the rich root of the cultivated olive tree.

Branches were broken off so that non-Jews might be grafted in; however, the Jews were broken off because of their unbelief, and non-Jews only stand through faith. And even the Jews, if they do not continue in their unbelief, they will be grafted back in, for God Almighty has the power and the will to graft them in again. And if non-Jews were cut from what is by nature a wild olive tree, and grafted, contrary to nature, into a cultivated olive tree, how much more easily will the natural branches be grafted back into their own olive tree. As said before, those branches of Israel that have been broken off, if they do not persist in their unbelief, will be grafted back in, for God Almighty has the power and will to graft them in again. For if non-Jews have been cut from what is by nature a wild olive tree and grafted, contrary to nature, into the Jews' cultivated olive tree, how much more will these natural Jewish branches be grafted back into their own olive tree.

Now, as regards the gospel of Yeshua (Jesus), the Jews are enemies for the sake of the non-Jews, but regarding election, they are beloved for the sake of their forefathers; for the gifts and the calling of God Almighty are irrevocable. For just as the non-Jews were at one time disobedient to God Almighty but have now received mercy because of the disobedience of the Jews, so they too have now been disobedient in order that by the mercy shown to the non-Jews they also may now receive mercy. God Almighty has consigned all to disobedience, that he may have mercy on all (Romans 11:2–32).

And I will pour on the house of David and on the inhabitants of Jerusalem the Spirit of grace and supplication; then they will look to Me whom they pierced. Yes, they will mourn for Him as one mourns for his only son, and grieve for Him as one grieves for a firstborn (Zechariah 12:10).

Remember that non-Jews were once separated from Yeshua (Jesus) the Messiah (Christ), excluded from citizenship in Israel and strangers to the covenants of promise, they had no hope and were without Almighty God in the world. But now in Messiah (Christ) those who were once far off have been brought near by the blood of Yeshua (Jesus). For he himself is our peace, who has made both Jew and non-Jew one and has broken down in his flesh the dividing wall of hostility. For he is our peace; in his flesh he has brought both groups—Jews and non-Jews—into one and has broken down the dividing wall, that is, the wall of hostility between them. Yeshua (Jesus) has abolished the law with its commandments and decrees, that he might create in himself one new man in place of the two, thus making peace, and that he might reconcile both groups to God the Father in one body through the cross, thereby putting to death that hostility through it (Ephesians 2:12–16).

When talking with Nicodemus, a ruler and leader of the Jews—who understood that Yeshua (Jesus) had come from God because of the signs that he did—Yeshua (Jesus) told him that he must be born again, from above:—

> *Jesus answered him, "In truth, I tell you, no one can see the kingdom of God without being born again, from above"* (John 3:3).

What Yeshua (Jesus) told Nicodemus two times is what he would say to everyone: *"You must be born again, from above."* We become "born again, from above" when we repent of sin and truly believe in our hearts that Yeshua (Jesus) is God Almighty's Son, who died, was buried, and who rose from the dead three days later.

> *For this is the will of my Father, that everyone who looks to the Son and believes in him should have eternal life, and I will raise him up on the last day* (John 6:40).

Being "born again, from above" is essential to receiving the Holy Spirit and becoming a new creation with eternal life: —

> *Neither circumcision nor uncircumcision counts for anything, but a new creation. For all those who walk by this rule, peace and mercy be upon them, and upon the whole Israel of God* (Galatians 6:15–16).

The first recorded words of John the Baptist's ministry was: *"**Repent**, for the kingdom of heaven is at hand!"* (Matthew 3:1).

Also the first recorded words of Yeshua's (Jesus') ministry was: *"**Repent**, for the kingdom of heaven is near"* (Matthew 4:17).

True repentance is the doorway to salvation—for Jew and non-Jew alike.

> *While God has overlooked the times of human ignorance, now He commands all people everywhere to **repent***
> (Acts 17:30).

Repentance and being "born again, from above" brings salvation and citizenship in the "Israel of God" for both Jews and non-Jews. Yeshua (Jesus) is the New Covenant that God Almighty promised to the Jews, which included a much needed heart of flesh and a new spirit: —

And I will give you a new heart, and a new spirit I will put within you. And I will remove the heart of stone from your flesh and give you a heart of flesh (Ezekiel 36:26).

Which is very telling: —

For if that first covenant had been faultless, there would have been no occasion to look for a second (Hebrews 8:7). In speaking of "a second covenant," He has made the first one obsolete. And what is obsolete and growing old will soon disappear (Hebrews 8:13).

Therefore he—Yeshua (Jesus)—is the mediator of a new covenant, so that those who are called may receive the promised eternal inheritance, since a death has occurred that redeems them from the transgressions committed under the first covenant (Hebrews 9:15).

And so all Israel will be saved; as it is written, "Out of Zion will come the Deliverer; he will banish ungodliness from Jacob" (Romans 11:26).

And so we wait with patience for the longed-for Second Coming of Yeshua (Jesus), which the Scriptures testify of: —

Behold he is coming with the clouds, and every eye will see him, even those who pierced him, and all peoples of the earth will mourn because of him. Even so. Amen
(Revelation 1:7).

For the Lord himself, with a cry of command, with the archangel's call and with the sound of God's trumpet, will descend from heaven, and the dead in Messiah (Christ) will rise first (1Thessalonians 4:16).

...when he comes in the glory of his Father with the holy angels (Mark 8:38).

However, we must, of necessity, undergo some changes before we are caught up to our great God and heavenly Father: —

> Flesh and blood cannot inherit the kingdom of God, nor can the perishable inherit the imperishable. There is a mystery which has been hidden from past ages: We will not all die, but we will all be changed, in a twinkling of an eye, at the last trumpet. For the trumpet will sound, and those dead in Messiah (Christ) will be raised imperishable, and we all will be changed. For this perishable body must put on imperishability, and this mortal body must put on immortality. When this perishable body puts on imperishability, and this mortal body puts on immortality, then the saying that is written will be fulfilled: —
> "Death has been swallowed up in victory"
> "O death, where is your victory? O death, where is your sting?" (1Corinthians 15:50–55),
>
> *The sting of death is sin, and the power of sin is the law. But thanks be to God, who gives us the victory through our Lord Yeshua (Jesus) the Messiah (Christ)*
> (1Corinthians 15:56).

There seems little doubt that God Almighty has purposed a time of repentance for the Jews who have so blatantly rejected Yeshua (Jesus), as Isaiah recorded for posterity: —

> *He is despised and rejected by men, a Man of sorrows and acquainted with pain. And we hid, as it were, our faces from him; he was despised, and we did not esteem him*
> (Isaiah 53:3).

The rejection of Yeshua (Jesus) has been ongoing for millennia, and perhaps, just perhaps, the eyes that were blind to God Almighty, the ears that were closed to Him, and the hearts that could never understand, because of God's punitive punishment

The great and terrible Day of the LORD

(Isaiah 6:9–10), will all be opened and they will be healed when they visibly see Yeshua (Jesus), their Messiah, descending from heaven at the end of the age:—

> *When the Lord Yeshua (Jesus) is revealed from heaven with his mighty angels in flaming fire, inflicting vengeance on those who do not know God Almighty and on those who do not obey the gospel of our Lord Yeshua (Jesus). These will suffer the punishment of eternal destruction, separated from the presence of the LORD and from the glory of his power* (2Thessalonians 1:7–9).

The above Scripture is not to be interpreted as eternal hell-fire, but the meting out of a merited desert and this penalty is shown here in some detail. Destruction means not 'annihilation' but complete ruin. It is the loss of all that makes life worth living, and coupled together with 'eternal' it means the opposite of eternal life.

> *See, I am coming quickly, and My reward is with Me, to give to every one according to his work. I am the Alpha and the Omega, the Beginning and the End, the First and the Last* (Revelation 22:12–13).

If, after digesting all of the above, the reader feels ready to meet the King, there is no room for complacency. All is not over until change comes to us with the last trump. Remember, we are in the great and terrible, long-drawn-out, day of God Almighty; and it is written by John the Revelator:—

> *Then I was given a reed like a measuring rod. And the angel stood, saying, "Rise and measure the temple of God, the altar, and those who worship there* (Revelation 11:1).

Now we know there is no physical temple in heaven. We, who truly believe in God Almighty's resurrected Son, are living stones *"being built together to become a dwelling in which God lives by his Spirit"* (Ephesians 2:22).

> *Do you not know that you are God's temple and that God's Spirit dwells in you?* (1Corinthians 3:16).

Therefore we shall all be measured, along with what we bring to the altar, by a divine measuring rod, which will see whether we are simply content at being while we wait for our change to come, or whether we will to do that which is pleasing to our God and King; it is what we do not do that is so displeasing to Him.

> *The conclusion of the matter, when all has been heard, is: fear God Almighty and keep His commandments, because this is the whole duty of every person*
>
> (Ecclesiasticus 12:13).

A test question was put to Yeshua (Jesus) by a lawyer:—

> Teacher, which is the greatest commandment in the law? He said to him, *"You shall love the LORD your God with all your heart, and with all your soul, and with all your mind. This is the greatest and first commandment. And a second is like it: 'You shall love your neighbor as yourself.' On these two commandments hang all the law and the prophets"* (Matthew 22:36–40).

Those who wish to please our God and Father and make Him smile should heed the words of Yeshua (Jesus):—

> *In everything, do to others what you would have them do to you, for this fulfills the Law and the Prophets*
>
> (Matthew 7:12).

Yeshua (Jesus) also said:—

> *My mother and my brothers are those who **hear** the word of God and **do** it* (Luke 2:21).

 Other Ramon Bennett books under *Shekinah* imprint

***When Day and Night Cease*:** A prophetic study of world events and how prophecy concerning Israel affects the nations, the Church and you

***SAGA*:** Israel and the demise of nations

***Philistine*:** The Great Deception

***The Wall*:** Prophecy, Politics and Middle East "Peace"

***The Wilderness*:** Israel's Ultimate Wandering

***GAZA*:** The Fallout From Premeditated Barbarianism

All My Tears (Ramon Bennett's auto biography)

Gospel (the four gospels blended into a single narrative)

No Other Name (the four blended gospels with some commentaries)

Abe (the life and example of Abraham, the father of faith)

My Cup Runneth Over (An ornate, cracked and chipped cup that was supernaturally made new again)

Apples Of Gold (Bible teaching on seventeen subjects)

to the jew first: *: however, the good news is for everyone*

***Mountains and Mulberry Trees*:** Going Forth in the Spirit and Power of Jesus

***HiSTORY*:** The Birth, Life, And Death of Jesus Christ, Son of God, Redeemer of Mankind

www.ingramcontent.com/pod-product-compliance
Lightning Source LLC
Chambersburg PA
CBHW060821050426
42453CB00008B/528